BOEING

Guy Norris and Mark Wagner

MBI Publishing Company

First published in 1998 by MBI Publishing Company, 729 Prospect Avenue, PO Box 1, Osceola, WI 54020-0001 USA

MBI Publishing Company books are also available at discounts in bulk quantity for industrial or sales-promotional use. For details write to Special Sales Manager at Motorbooks International Wholesalers & Distributors, 729 Prospect Avenue, PO Box 1, Osceola, WI 54020-0001 USA.

Library of Congress Cataloging-in-Publication Data
Norris, Guy.
       Boeing / Guy Norris & Mark Wagner.
          p. cm.
       Includes index.
       ISBN 0-7603-0497-1 (alk. paper)
       1. Boeing airplanes--History. 2. Boeing Company--History.
     I. Wagner, Mark, 1964- II. Title.
     TL686.B65N665 1998
     338.7'62913334--dc21   98-24792

On the front cover: The enormous triple-slotted flaps of the 747 were based on technology developed for the 727. Sophisticated high-lift devices were an essential element of the 747, which was designed to use the same length runways as 707s and DC-8s.

On the frontispiece: The only visible difference in the flight deck between the -200 and the -300 is the use of one of the multifunction screens to display pictures from the ground maneuver camera system, and the small control panel to control the system. The split-screen image, visible above the throttle quadrant, shows the view from each of the three cameras. One is located beneath the forward fuselage to view the nose wheel while the others view the main gear wheels from their mountings in the leading edge of the horizontal stabilizer.

On the title page: A United 747-400 touches down. Like the previous generations before it, the large wing area, huge flaps, and multiple undercarriage combined to provide a cushioning effect, which helped make most landings trouble-free. Note the spoilers deploying as touchdown occurs. The crew begins to flare the 747 gently at around 50 feet and begins closing the throttles at 30 feet while holding the stick back slightly against any nose-down pitch motion. By 10 feet, with power at idle, the 747 mushes into a ground-effect cushion of its own creation.

On the back cover, top: Subtle aerodynamic differences can be seen in the thicker root of the Next Generation's advanced wing. Note also the wider span of the horizontal stabilizer and the wide-chord fan blades of the CFM56-7B engine.

On the back cover, bottom: The famous P-26 combined the new streamlined benefits of the monoplanes with a few of the more durable features of the older biplane generation, such as the wire-braced wings, open cockpit and fixed landing gear. This is the P-26 prototype, the XP-936, pictured at Boeing Field three days before its first flight on March 20, 1932.

Edited by Mike Haenggi
Designed by Katie L. Sonmor

Printed in Hong Kong through World Print, Ltd.

Contents

Acknowledgments

We are indebted to the many Boeing employees, past and present, who provided so much advice, assistance, and guidance to help bring this book to life. Thanks to Joe Sutter, Brigadier General Guy Townsend USAF (Ret), Brien Wygle, and William Cook who shared pioneering experiences and the insight of designers and test pilots. Grateful thanks particularly to Mike Lombardi and Tom Lubbesmeyer without whose exceptional archive knowledge this book would not have been possible. Also Bill Cogswell, Tony McArthy, Debbie Nomaguchi, Fred Solis, Doug Webb, and Leslie Wilder who gave so much time during a busy period. From the Douglas Products Division, we would also like to thank Don Hanson, Warren Lamb, Barbara Raines, and Bob Saling. Special appreciation to Brian Baum of the Seattle Museum of Flight, Rick Kennedy of General Electric, and Mark Sullivan of Pratt & Whitney for help, contacts, and encouragement. Thanks to Tim Chopp of the Berlin Airlift Historical Foundation, David Drimmer, Vince Fleming, Robert L. Frelow, John A. Lewandowski, Michael Marek, David Messing, and Frank B. Mormillo. For B-29 memories, thanks to Bob Madden, Cindy Siriani, and Col. Dave Weisman USAF (Ret). Thanks to Bill Ried, Col. Donald R. Davis, Col. Neal Harrison, Cols. Russ and Betty Anderson, Paul Koskela, Jerome A. Flesher, C. Eric Ray, John R. Deakin, and all at the Confederate Air Force. Thanks also to John Bailey, John Braden, Lucy Bristow, Austin Brown, Philip Bruce, Gareth Burgess, Charles Cannon, Benjamin Chan, Tony S. K. Chan, Brian Cheung, Anthony Concil, Don Dick, Steve Dudley, Kimberly Foster, Capt. Ian Johnson, Steve Klodt, Kensuke Kotera, Hideaki Kuroki, Jenny P. S. Lei, Capt. Mike Livesey, Rosana Maniquis, Peter R. March, Andy Marsh; Leo, Sandi, and Megan Mitchell; Kate Morris; Greg, Judy, and Tom Norris; Jim Reynolds, Darren Roberts, Hiroshi Sakatsume, Naoya Sato, A. A. Scheel, Pat Schoneberger, Hiroshi Shimada, Richard Siegel, Andy Smith, Bryan Southgate, Tetsuhisa Sugano, Hernando Vergara, Tom Winfrey, Anthony Won, and Katsuhiko Yumino. Thanks also to the staff of Flight International, particularly Paul Lewis, Graham Warwick, and Allan Winn. Our sincere thanks to our editor at MBI Publishing Company, Michael Haenggi.
—*Guy Norris & Mark Wagner*

Introduction

This is an aeronautical detective story. It traces the fascinating, and sometimes surprising, evidence that links Boeing's present jetliner family with its venerable forebears. Side by side, there seems to be little in common between the enormous 747 and Boeing's very early, fragile floatplanes. Other than their maker's name, most people assume that virtually the only characteristic they share is their ability to fly. Yet the truth is very different. Even Boeing's most recent aircraft have links to the past that reveal an intriguing tale of design evolution.

The detective work has been helped by Boeing's unique status as the only U.S. aircraft manufacturer to have remained in continuous operation for more than 80 years. This solid lineage has ensured a rich network of threads that bind Boeing's designs together across the decades. Some of these threads are easy to trace, for example, the swept wing of the B-47 and its dramatic influence on all subsequent Boeing jetliner designs. Other threads, such as the development of a simpler arc-welding manufacturing process for rebuilt deHavilland DH-4s and Boeing's own Model 15 fighter, are relatively obscure but had profound downstream effects. Similarly, even the little known influence of one-off designs such as the enormous XB-15 bomber on Boeing's flight deck and systems heritage are often overlooked and need more spade work to unearth.

This book explains some of these connections and reveals the impact of both preceding designs and even non-Boeing designs on successive generations. As it focuses on the generic trail of the company's fixed-wing family, it does not deal with the various off-shoots of Boeing's ever widening product range. Helicopters, missiles, space vehicles, hydrofoils, and the products of Boeing's latest acquisitions, Rockwell North American and McDonnell Douglas, are therefore not included, except in cases where competing designs had a profound influence on Boeing's fixed-wing family.

Boeing's ability to learn from the past has helped it time and again to overcome challenges that have defeated lesser companies. The philosophy of "lessons learned" is as much a part of the current Boeing design process as the engineers, designers and aerodynamics specialists who implement it. This book provides a glimpse of the "lessons learned" process at work over the ages and sets the stage for the next generation of Boeing designs as it moves into the twenty-first century. With more than 80 years of design heritage under its belt, the company is well prepared for the challenges of the next century.

Fifty years after the fragile B&W launched the Boeing dynasty, a replica of Model 1 is pictured flying high over Lake Washington in 1966. The design was strongly influenced by Boeing's experiences with seaplanes built by Glenn L. Martin. *Boeing*

1
Floatplanes to Fighters

No one watching the frail wood and fabric floatplane alight gently on Seattle's Lake Union that summer day in June 1916 could possibly have realized that this was the birth of an aeronautical colossus. The twin-pontoon biplane was piloted by its co-developer, William E. Boeing, and was the first member of a family of aircraft that one day would come to dominate air transport, deliver the winning blow in a world war, safeguard peace, and build prosperity for millions.

The B&W Model 1 was named after Boeing and his joint venture partner, Commander G. Conrad Westervelt of the U.S. Navy. The two friends had become passionate over the new craze of flying and, together with Herb Munter, a pioneering pilot from the area, formed the Aero Club of Seattle. Boeing was a successful local businessman dealing in the thriving timber industry and was wealthy enough to learn to fly and buy a Glenn L. Martin seaplane in 1915. The single-float aircraft formed the core of the new club. Fortunately for the course of aviation history, it was damaged in an accident.

The incident was all the pair needed. Boeing and Westervelt had already convinced themselves they could build something better and, unimpressed by the time it would take to get new parts for the Martin, took the bold step to have a go at making their own aircraft. Westervelt contacted friends in the Navy Department to help with the project. Thanks mainly to the efforts of Glenn Martin, who had made the first successful flight of his own seaplane in January 1912, the Navy was beginning to see the potential of aircraft for over-the-horizon scouting and patrol missions. As a result, the Navy was keeping close watch on developments at the Massachusetts Institute of Technology (M.I.T) where most of the first organized aerodynamic research in the country was concentrated. A bright M.I.T aerodynamicist named Jerome Hunsaker passed on valuable data to the inexperienced designer, and Model 1 began to take shape.

Boeing's Martin machine heavily influenced the Model 1 design. Construction of some parts took place at the Heath Shipyard, situated on the banks of the Duwamish River in Seattle where William Boeing's yacht had been built. Ed Heath, a skilled boat builder, made the twin pontoons. Sub-assemblies were transported from there to a small hangar that Boeing had made to house the Martin on the shores of Lake Union. The fuselage, with forc-and-aft seating for two, was made in the hangar where it was mated with the wings and floats. In common with current practice, the skeletal structure was made from wood and formed what was basically an "N-type" girder structure. Four main longitudinal members known as longerons formed the overall rectangular cross-section. The whole structure was braced with piano wire and covered with fabric that was made taut by brushing with cellulose dope.

The symmetrical lines of the B&W are clearly demonstrated in this view of the replica aircraft suspended from the roof of the Seattle Museum of Flight. Note the craftsmanship of the wooden floats, which, like those of the original, were made by boat builders.

The Hall Scott Motor Car Company, which helped develop the successful Liberty engine with Packard for the last year of World War I, provided its simple, inline A-5 engine. This was rated at 125 horsepower and turned a two-blade wooden propeller. The engine was started by compressed air stored in a tank behind the second cockpit and controlled with a foot pedal like an automobile accelerator. This was later changed to a hand control along with the flight control system, which did not originally use rudder pedals. Instead, the aircraft was controlled by a single inceptor that combined all the flying surfaces. Forward movement of the control column regulated pitch by moving the elevators up and down as did side-to-side movement, which operated the large wing tip ailerons. The major difference was the rudder,

which was linked to a control wheel on top of the column rather than to rudder pedals.

The first aircraft, named Bluebell, made its maiden flight with Boeing at the controls on June 29, 1916. By the time the second aircraft, named Mallard, flew in November, the face of the fledgling operation had already changed. Westervelt, whom the U.S. Navy had posted to Bremerton Naval shipyard, was recalled to the East Coast and did not even get to see the first flight. With the loss of Westervelt, Boeing moved to re-establish a fresh identity and formed the Pacific Aero Products Company, which was incorporated on July 15, 1916.

The young company suffered its first setback when the slightly unstable B&W failed to clinch a production order from the U.S. Navy. In response, Boeing appointed a gifted M.I.T graduate, Tsu Wong, to improve the design. The revised aircraft was built to be inherently stable with a pronounced wing stagger and noticeable dihedral, or upward canting, of the wings. The fixed horizontal stabilizer of the B&W was deleted, only the large elevator retained, and a vertical fin was added. Boeing considered the Model 2, as it was called, the first "real" all-new Boeing design because the B&W had borrowed so much from the Martin configuration. The Model 2 was designated the C-4 because it was the third design and the fourth aircraft under Boeing ownership, including the original seaplane. As it was the third aircraft actually made by the firm, it was serial number three.

Unfortunately the C-4 had several flaws, most of which were caused by a lack of lateral and pitch stability due to the small tail area. A larger rudder was installed, and on April 19, 1917, the aircraft was successfully test flown by Munter. Two more C aircraft, designated Model 3s, were built for U.S. Navy trials as potential trainers. The future of Boeing's company hinged on the success of the trials at the Pensacola Naval Air Station in Florida. The two Model 3 aircraft were only slightly different from the Model 2 in that the center struts joined over the fuselage. The aircraft was powered by a 100-horsepower Hall-Scott A-7A engine, which was distinguished by two side-mounted water-cooling radiators in place of the single front radiator of the Model 1. The trainer was also more compact than the Model 1 with a 9-foot-smaller span of 43 feet 10 inches and a length of 27 feet compared to the 31-foot, 2-inch length of the first aircraft.

To Boeing's delight, the U.S. Navy ordered 50 as primary trainers, formally launching the company into

a money-making business with a $575,000 contract. The aircraft were called Model Cs by Boeing but were officially designated as Model 5s. The "missing" Model 4 was a landplane version of the Model 3 with wheels and side-by-side seating. The two Model 4s built (with the designation E, the fifth letter of the alphabet, for the number of aircraft, and A for Army, for which they were designed), were distinguished by an unusual third undercarriage leg that was positioned well forward of the main wheels. Although it resembled the nose-leg of a tricycle gear arrangement, the extra wheel was designed to prevent the all-too-frequent occurrence of nosing over on landing. The Model 4 was Boeing's first landplane and the first to use, in this case, a 100-horse-power Curtiss OXX-3 rather than a Hall-Scott engine. The two aircraft were handed over to the Army in January 1917, but no further examples were built.

The U.S. Navy contract coincided with yet more changes for the firm, which was renamed the Boeing Airplane Company. Wong resigned, leaving Boeing to find a replacement at a critical time. The Model C contract had been spurred by America's entry into World War I and business was booming. New recruits included two young University of Washington graduates, Clairmont Egtvedt and Philip Johnson. Both would ultimately become presidents of the company, Egtvedt going down in history as the father of the four-engined bomber through his involvement in the birth of the B-17.

Boeing
developed a new arc-welding process to make the steel-tube fuselages of the DH-4M-1s, which it rebuilt for the Army Air Service. The use of stronger steel-tube construction methods, seen clearly in the foreground, was prompted by postwar inspections of similarly built German Fokker D.VIIs. *Boeing*

Boeing-modified
DH-4 "Liberty Planes," based on a
re-engined version of the British-
designed deHavilland 4, were used
to carry airmail in the early 1920s.
The need for a replacement led to
the design of Boeing's Model 40
and, in doing so, planted the seeds
for the company's first airliners.

Like many other aircraft companies, Boeing was contracted by the Navy to build the popular Curtiss HS-2L
patrol flying boats. The company's existing float-making
techniques were ideally suited to the construction of the
flying boat's wooden hull, but the new knowledge gained
was invaluable to Boeing's immediate postwar designs, the
B-1 and BB-1. Unfortunately for Boeing, the war ended
and the contract was canceled after only half of the 50
HS-2Ls on order had been built.

Boeing's fortunes dipped dramatically with the
armistice. Military work vanished, and what little
growth there was in the fledgling civil market was swal-
lowed whole by the widespread availability of cheap,
war-surplus aircraft that, in most cases, were still in their
packing crates. The only good news was the sale of the
first two B&Ws to the New Zealand government—Boe-

ing's first international customer—for airmail duties.
The notion of airmail carriers appealed to Boeing as a
potential market for his aircraft closer to home. Within
months of the sale of the B&Ws, he and Edward Hubbard flew a modified Model C on a demonstration international airmail flight from Vancouver to Seattle in
March 1919. Boeing then combined the idea of the
Model C airmail flight with the improved utility of the
Curtiss HS-2L and came up with his first commercial
design—the Model 6, B-1 pusher flying boat.

The B-1 was shorter and stockier than the Curtiss flying boat, with reduced span length and a narrower hull. A
slight degree of stagger was also introduced to the upper
wing, which was of a marginally lower aspect ratio compared to the slender, 74-foot, 1-inch span of the HS-2L.
Eddie Hubbard bought the first model in 1920 and used

it continuously for eight years on the Seattle to Victoria airmail route. In this period the original 200-horsepower Hall-Scott L-6 was replaced by a 400-horsepower, 12-cylinder Liberty. In all, just nine B-1s were built.

Hubbard's lone B-1 flew on for nine years before new versions, designated the B-1D and 1E, were built. Outwardly resembling the original pusher design, these later versions were so different in detail that they were actually considered entirely new designs. The hull structure, for example, was made up of wooden longerons covered with strips of spruce veneer. Even the wings were quite different, being made of panels from the Model 40 described later. Performance was also improved in these later versions with the availability of the 410-horsepower Pratt & Whitney Wasp. By 1929 Boeing developed a fifth seat for the aircraft and decided it was, therefore, time to redesignate the flying boat the Model 204. The second factory-made 204 was built as a dual-control aircraft for William Boeing himself, and later continued the Seattle–Victoria international airmail contract originally signed by Hubbard. Four Model 204s were also built by Boeing-Canada, the boat maker's first aircraft, and designated C-204 Thunderbirds.

Two spin-off designs emerged from the B-1. The Model 7 BB-1 flew for the first time that year and was a scaled-down variant aimed mainly at the sports market. The wing shape and engine of the BB-1 were, in turn, used on a landplane called the Model 8, BB-L6. The design differed from previous Boeing aircraft in having a mahogany plywood fuselage skin. The fuselage cross-section was also made up using three longerons instead of the more conventional four-piece rectangular arrangement.

While all the new designs were good, none of them sold. The market was still saturated with war-surplus equipment, and by 1920, Boeing's losses reached $300,000. In the bleak postwar recession years, the company even turned to bedroom furniture manufacturing and the assembly of speedboats called "sea sleds" to make ends meet. Salvation arrived in the form of new military contracts to make or modernize other manufacturers' aircraft. Chief among these were the Thomas Morse MB-3A and deHavilland DH-4. As the lowest bidder, Boeing worked a $1,448,000 deal to build 200 MB-3As, a conventional single-seat, biplane fighter. Although the aircraft were all delivered between 1921 and late 1922, the MB-3A provided vital work in a lean period and, most important of all, gave Boeing invaluable experience that would later lead to its domination of the U.S. fighter scene until the late 1930s.

The DH-4 work involved rebuilding several hundred of the British-designed "Liberty Planes" for the Army Air Service. Although the first 111 were upgraded with minor improvements, the big modification was made with subsequent contracts when more than 180 DH-4s were rebuilt with steel-tube fuselages. The benefits of this construction technique had become apparent when the United States had the chance to inspect German Fokker D.VII fighters at the end of the war. Compared to the braced woodwork structure of the Allied aircraft, the steel-tubed Fokkers were stronger, more durable, and much easier to maintain. The latter half of the DH-4 contract was therefore aimed at incorporating these benefits into the fleet. To speed up the fuselage manufacturing, Boeing developed an arc-welding process to join the complex tubing rather than using the slower gas-welding alternative. This advanced

The Model 15 broke new ground for American fighter design with its tapered wings and recessed engine-cooling radiator. Boeing's big gamble on the XPW-9 (Experimental Pursuit, Water-Cooled Design Number 9) paid off handsomely leading to a decade of fighter-building dominance. Note the wire bracing in the wooden wings and steel-tube fuselage. Peeping into the background is the nose section of the unsuccessful GA-2 ground attack aircraft. *Boeing*

Of

the 123 PW-9s ordered by the Army, 40 were PW-9Cs like the example pictured above. This state-of-the-art fighter for 1926 was powered by a water-cooled Curtiss D-12D, armed with two machine guns, and could carry two 122-pound bombs. *Boeing*

electrically based process laid the foundation for mass-production techniques that would become vital to Boeing's efficiency in future years.

Another military contract that helped keep Boeing afloat was a relatively huge, ungainly attack aircraft dubbed the GA-X (ground attack experimental). Built to an Army design, the Model 10, GA-1 was Boeing's only triplane and its first multi-engined program. Unfortunately, it was so heavily armored that the twin 435-horsepower Liberty 12As could barely cope. The armor-protected gunners fired forward from positions mounted in front of the pusher engines. Slots with shutters were provided for the gunners and the pilot, who consequently had very limited

visibility. To the relief of pilots, the contract was cut from 20 to 10, though the small fleet soldiered on for years from its base at Kelly Field, Texas. An attempt to revive the aircraft as the redesigned GA-2 failed when testing proved it to be impractical.

FIGHTER FAMILY

Boeing engineers and designers gained confidence as well as experience by making other people's aircraft. At the same time they also began to see the shortcomings of these designs. As a result, a team led by Egtvedt began working on an all-new fighter design that used many of the novel European design and construction techniques. Although Boeing was not working to a specific U.S. military requirement and was therefore taking a risk with the company-sponsored project, it was also free of the traditional design "guidelines" normally imposed by the government. This meant Egtvedt's team was free to exploit recent breakthroughs in materials and design technology and produce what the members believed would be a contract-winning design.

They were right. The first design produced by this method, the Model 15, went on to win orders in various versions (notably the PW-9 and FB-1) and led to Boeing's dominance of the U.S. fighter market for more than a

By

the start of the 1930s the "100 Series" exemplified Boeing's expertise in biplane fighters. The "100 Series" and its directly related F4B and P-12 sister aircraft formed the U.S. military's last front-line biplane forces. Although painted up as an externally identical P-12, this is actually the second of four Model 100s built as commercial versions of the F4B. It served with Pratt & Whitney as a testbed for Wasp and Hornet engines before beginning a new career as an air-show performer in the hands of stunt pilot Milo Burcham. It later starred in films like *Task Force* before eventually passing into the co-ownership of Lew Wallick, chief test pilot for the 727.

decade. Most of the secret lay in the use of steel tubing for the fuselage structure and the design of much thicker wing sections made from wood. As with the DH-4 rebuild before it, many of these lessons were learned from the design of the Fokker D.VII.

The wing design was particularly interesting as it was thick and did not follow the increasing trend toward thinner, lower-drag aerofoils. While this cross-section appeared to be a step backwards, it allowed the structure to be made from rugged, cantilevered box spars. In terms of performance, the thick wing produced lots of lift, even at relatively high altitudes, and had only a slight effect on top speed. The wing spars were made with spruce and strengthened with mahogany webs, while the ribs, laid transversely between the spars, were made from three-ply wood reinforced with spruce. The wing shape, although originally intended to be straight chord, ultimately went to a taper planform. The final design, which emerged in January 1922, also reintroduced some wire bracing into the wing, which was modified from full-cantilever to semi-cantilever.

Despite its open reliance on the Fokker design, the Model 15 featured some notable home improvements. The Boeing-developed arc-welding process, for example, simplified the manufacture of the steel-tubed fuselage. The design also featured an adjustable tailplane that could be altered in flight to help trim the aircraft. This particular development would again come to the fore in the 1950s and 1960s with the "flying tail" of the B-52 and 707. Another new aspect was the unusual positioning of the radiator, away from the usual flat-plate location in the nose of the aircraft to a recessed area beneath the engine.

By mid-1923, the first aircraft, now dubbed the XPW-9 (P for Pursuit) was undergoing military testing, and within 14 months, the first orders for PW-9s were rolling in. The Navy was also impressed by the new little Boeing aircraft and began receiving the first FB-1s, as they were called, in 1925. The 32-foot-span aircraft had an impressive top speed of 160 miles per hour and an equally head-turning rate of climb of 1,630 feet per minute. It could also pack a punch with one 30 caliber machine gun and one 55 caliber machine gun, or two 30s. In addition, it was fitted to carry two 122-pound bombs.

Various improvements were made to increase the aircraft's capabilities and survivability. These included a new fire extinguisher system, better brakes, a more efficient radiator, and a bigger rudder to improve the usual Boeing shortcoming of inadequate directional stability. The biggest improvements of all began to emerge in the mid-

The gleaming metallic fuselage and tail surfaces of the P-12E illustrate the next advance in fighter design. The P-12E was the first production model of the P-12/F4B series to use the stronger semi-monocoque fuselage and larger tail surfaces introduced experimentally on the Model 218. This aircraft is preserved at the Planes of Fame Museum in Chino, California, and is painted in U.S. Navy colors to represent the virtually identical F4B-3.

1920s with the availability of newer, more powerful engines. The Model 55, or FB-3, was essentially a derivative of the FB-2 fitted with a 510-horsepower Packard 1A-1500. The FB-2 was a modified FB-1 with changes to the gear to accommodate an arrestor hook for carrier landings. The Packard was a large, water-cooled V-12, which was housed in a streamlined nacelle, allowing the attainment of higher speeds of up to 180 miles per hour. The most dramatic engine change, however, came with the arrival of the radial, air-cooled engines such as Pratt & Whitney's classic R-1340 "Wasp" and Wright's P-1, the 450 horsepower predecessor of the Wright Cyclone.

The Wasp was first designed and produced in 1925. It was manufactured for 36 years, with a staggering 34,966 engines built. The nine-cylinder piston quickly established itself as a truly reliable powerplant, and the Navy was so impressed that it made the Wasp standard for all ship-based aircraft and withdrew all liquid-cooled engines from service by 1928. The period gave Pratt & Whitney its reputation as the manufacturer of "Dependable Engines," a phrase used as the company's marketing slogan ever since.

The Packard engine continued to feature heavily in Boeing designs, however, and in its 600-horsepower 2A-1500 form was used, inverted, as the powerplant for the Model 66, or XP-8. This was Boeing's response to an Air Corps specification issued in 1925 and followed the PW-9/FB lineage in most respects. The wing configuration was changed to increase stability around the roll axis with the span of the lower wing set extended by 2 feet and the span of the upper wings reduced by the same amount to 30 feet, 1 inch. Oleo-pneumatic shock absorbers that had been introduced on the FB-2 were also incorporated and became standard on every Boeing fighter that followed.

One specific victim of the Navy's new love affair with the Wasp was Boeing's next venture, the Model 67, or FB-5. The aircraft was essentially a production version of the FB-3 with increased wing stagger and a completely new, beefed-up landing gear for high-speed impact on carrier decks. Its only major drawback, as far as the Navy was concerned, was its liquid-cooled Packard 2A-1500 engine. Although all 27 built were delivered by January 1927, they were retired within three years as the Wasp-powered aircraft took over.

Boeing recognized the trend just as quickly and began studying a re-engined version of the FB-5 called the FB-7. The scheme soon died as Navy interest switched to another Boeing design, the Model 69, which was built around a combination of the new P&W engine and the revised aerodynamics of the Model 66. The Model 69 was tested by the Navy as the XF2B-1 in November 1926; this quickly led to an order for 32 production versions called the F2B-1. Powered by the 425-horsepower version of the Wasp, the F2B-1 had a maximum speed of 158 miles per hour and a ceiling of 21,500 feet. It established a reputation for clean, crisp handling and was used by the Three Sea Hawks, the U.S. Navy's first aerobatic display team, the forerunners of today's Blue Angels. The F2B-1 also saw the first notable use of a new fuselage construction technique in which the tubes forming the framework were bolted together rather than welded.

Encouraged by its success, Boeing developed another aircraft for the Navy as a private venture. Unfortunately, the hopes pinned on the Model 74, or XF3B-1, did not

PT-13As,
better known as the Stearman Model 75 Kaydet, formed the backbone of Army training. Here an impressive line-up awaits inspection under a hot midday sun at Alancock Field, Santa Maria, California, in the fall of 1939. *Boeing*

Radials
versus inline, air-cooled versus liquid-cooled. The second Wasp-powered Model 40A nears completion in 1927 opposite a row of PW-9 fuselages and their Curtiss D-12 engines. The Wasp transformed the performance of the Model 40, helping Boeing win the airmail bid and reinforcing the trend toward the new radial engines for all new aircraft. *Boeing*

amount to a production order, but they did result in new advances that helped the company in years to come. The XF3B-1 looked very similar to the early F2B-1 but with an undercarriage similar to the FB-5. In this configuration, the strut was attached to the fuselage at the front lower wing spar fitting, providing greater strength for carrier landings. The aircraft flew in March 1927 but did not impress the Navy enough to warrant a production contract. Boeing took back the biplane and modified it into virtually a new aircraft.

One of the most significant alterations to the Model 77, or F3B-1 as the new aircraft was called, was to the upper wing. This was altered with a constant chord and a sweepback angle of almost 6.5 degrees while the lower wing had no sweep angle at all and a constant chord. Significantly, for the first time the tail surfaces were all metal rather than the traditional fabric-covered construction of previous models. This produced a much stiffer surface, and it was featured on every subsequent Boeing biplane fighter. The redesign was much more successful, and the Navy ordered 73 (excluding the prototype), all of which were delivered by the end of 1928.

Even as the F3B-1 was being readied for production, Boeing was hard at work on yet another privately funded gamble. This was the Model 83, an advanced biplane that the company hoped would become a next-generation successor to the Army's PW-9 as well as the Navy's F2Bs and even its relatively new F3Bs. Although nothing was radically new about their designs, the Model 83, and its virtually identical sister aircraft, the Model 89, proved to be the right aircraft at the right time. They coincided with the start of the monoplane fighter era yet were neither too ambitiously futuristic nor too old-fashioned. Ultimately they led to the P-12, F4B, and 100 series of Boeing fighters. In all, a total of 586 were produced.

The new models were instantly distinguished from earlier Boeing biplanes by having straight rather than tapered wings. The wings were built in the same way as the preceding types with two box spar construction, while the tail surfaces and ailerons were made using the now standard, semi-monocoque (stressed skin) corrugated dural method. The structure of the fuselage was also made up of bolted square section aluminum tubing in the manner of the F2B-1 and subsequent aircraft. The use of aluminum meant reduced weight, which equated to higher speed. The Model 83 flew in June 1928, while the Model 89, which differed in having a tripod undercarriage arrangement, flew

The
extra power of the 525-horsepower
P&W Hornet allowed the Model
40B-4 to carry up to 4 passengers,
500 pounds of mail and—on a good
day like the one pictured—reach its
service ceiling of just over 16,000 feet.
Boeing

An
early Model 80A comes together in
July 1929. Note the intricate welded
steel-tube truss structure of the wing
and the close positioning of the two
main spars. Notice also the P&W
Hornet engines and the bolted
square aluminum tubing construction
of the rear fuselage. *Boeing*

in August that year. Trials led to a production order of 27 F4B-1s for the Navy. These were designated with the Boeing model number 99 and were also produced in civil guise as the Model 100. In addition, the Army ordered a version that became the P-12B but which Boeing called the Model 102.

Continuous improvements were introduced to keep the P-12/F4B series as up to date as possible. These included the introduction of a semi-monocoque metal fuselage structure, a low drag ring cowl over the engine, improved ailerons, and revised tail surfaces. Later models also had an enlarged headrest that was contoured into the spine of the fuselage, providing stowage space for a life raft. The P-12/F-4Bs soldiered on through the 1930s and even into the 1940s when some surviving P-12s were even used as radio-controlled target aircraft by the Navy.

With the emergence of monoplanes, the era of the front-line biplane drew rapidly to a close in the 1930s. In the area of training, however, it continued to reign supreme and none more so than Boeing's famous Model 75 Kaydet. Better known as the Stearman after the small Boeing subsidiary that developed it, the solid primary trainer was built in huge numbers. The entire production run of the Model 70 to 75 series totaled a staggering 10,346 aircraft. This included spares that could be assembled into aircraft.

The new biplane was introduced at a perilous time for all U.S. manufacturers. The Depression was biting hard, and factories were closing down as work dried up. Stearman founder Lloyd Stearman gambled on a simple,

basically traditional design that was aimed at a large U.S. Army and Navy training requirement. The original Model 70 was powered by a 215-horsepower Lycoming radial and was designed and constructed using combined methods derived from Stearman's own experiences and those of his parent company, Boeing. The fuselage structure, for example,

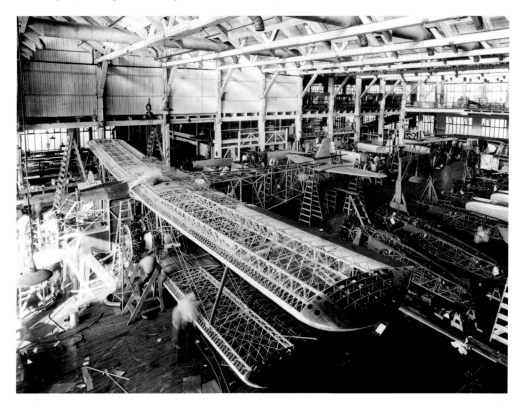

Pilots

sat in the unaccustomed luxury of an enclosed cockpit in the Model 80A. Only the captain (left seat) has full flight instruments while the engine parameters are indicated in triplicate in the center of the console. The last of the 12 original 80As was redesignated an -80B and built with an open cockpit after some of the pilots complained about the enclosed cockpit. After a couple of winters it was reconverted with the covered cockpit!

was made of welded steel tubing, while the wings were fabric-covered wood. It also had aerodynamically cleaner, single-piece undercarriage legs.

Following its construction in 1933, the Model 70 was tested by the military and in 1934 won an initial order from the U.S. Navy for 61 production versions dubbed the Model 73. The Navy replaced the Lycoming with the older Wright J-5 Whirlwind engine because it had lots of them in stock at the time. The Lycoming reappeared, however, when the Army placed the first of many thousands of orders for the trainer in 1935. Known to the Army as PT-13, -17, -18, and -27 (and N25 to the Navy), the production version was the Model 75 Kaydet, which was made in huge numbers. Many were exported to foreign air forces and were used as trainers (sometimes armed) by Argentina, Brazil, Canada, China, Great Britain, and the Philippines.

More than 4,000 Model 75s were still in widespread use after World War II, many of them re-engined with the 450-horsepower P&W Wasp Junior. Most ended up crop dusting well into the early 1970s when the gradual introduction of purpose-built agricultural aircraft such as the

Air Tractor and Ayres Thrush began to displace them. The high historic value of the Model 75 ensures that many continue to survive as collector's items to this day.

MAILPLANES AND MONOPLANES

In 1927, a rare combination of events coincided to put Boeing on the commercial aircraft map for the first time. The U.S. Post Office decided to privatize its transcontinental airmail service and invited bids from industry. Boeing, which had designed a big biplane called the Model 40 two years earlier for just such a contract, was waiting in the wings with a purpose-made design.

What made the huge difference in 1927, however, was the availability of the new P&W Wasp engine. Because of its experience with the XF2B-1 fighter, Boeing was quickly convinced that it had a winning engine on its hands. With at least a 200-pound payload gain to be had by using the Wasp in place of the World War I Liberty engine originally designed for the Model 40, Boeing's mind was made up. The winning solution was obviously a Model 40 re-engined with the new P&W powerplant.

The ultimate corporate transport of the early 1930s was this Model 226, belonging to the Standard Oil Company of California. Like the Model 80As, of which it was one of the original production batch, the lone 226 was fitted with auxiliary rudders and vertical fins. The specially appointed cabin contained six big armchairs, two foldaway beds, picture windows, deluxe upholstery, a sink, refrigerator, and even an oven. Note the copilot's relaxed posture as the aircraft formates for an air-to-air photo shoot over California. *Boeing*

There was one other problem to overcome, however. The runaway success of the Wasp meant the engine was in short supply. Production was committed to supplying the new fighters rolling off the production lines for the U.S. Navy. It was only William Boeing's personal friendship with the P&W president, Frederick Renschler, that enabled a deal to be struck with the Navy that allowed some engines to be diverted to the improved Model 40A, as the upgraded derivative was called.

Boeing's luck in securing the engines prevailed and, having won its bid for the San Francisco–Chicago leg of the airmail route, it began operations with the new Model 40A in July 1927. The large biplane could take up to 1,200 pounds of mail as well as two passengers who were accommodated in a tiny cabin forward of the cockpit. This novel feature created new opportunities to make money on the route and was another reason for Boeing's successful bid. During the first year of operation, the aircraft carried 1,863 passengers who each paid $400 to fly. While the passengers sat snugly in the cabin, the pilot, meanwhile, remained exposed to the elements. While the configuration offered some new features, the structure of the 40A

High tea at 8,000 feet. Although others had employed male stewards, Boeing Air Transport was the first to hire female cabin attendants. The original eight "stewardesses" to work the Model 80A fleet were registered nurses from hospitals in Chicago and San Francisco. *Boeing*

borrowed heavily from the techniques developed for the fighters. The fuselage structure was made from welded steel throughout, while the 44-foot, 2 1/4-inch span wings and tail were of conventional wood construction.

Boeing even formed its own airline, Boeing Air Transport, to run the new operation, and by the end of the following year it had acquired Pacific Air Transport (PAT)

to expand its operations. Much bigger changes were just around the corner and, shortly after the purchase of PAT was completed, Boeing itself became part of the giant new United Aircraft and Transport Corporation. The immense holding company, with headquarters in Hartford, Connecticut, owned all the capital stock of Boeing, Boeing Air Transport, and PAT. Other companies under the United umbrella included Chance Vought Corporation, Pratt & Whitney, and Hamilton Aero Manufacturing Company, a successful propeller maker. Later additions included Sikorsky Aviation Corporation, the Stearman Aircraft Company of Kansas, and the Standard Steel Propeller company that later merged with Hamilton to form today's Hamilton Standard.

The airline operation grew at the same time to include operators such as Stout Airlines, National Air Transport, and Varney Air Lines. Growth was so dramatic that a new management company called United Airlines was formed to run the operation, even though each carrier retained its original identity.

Model 40 developments continued, but Boeing's growing airline involvement quickly convinced it that a larger, purpose-made passenger aircraft would be viable.

This included first-hand experience of aircraft such as the Fokker Trimotor, which was flown by some of its newly acquired airlines. In 1928, it therefore decided to go ahead with a 12-seater trimotor design called the Model 80. This large, 80-foot-span aircraft used wing construction methods first developed for a flying boat called the Model 50, or PB-1. This was designed in 1924 in response to a U.S. Navy requirement for a long-range patrol aircraft capable of flying nonstop for the 2,400-mile route from Hawaii to San Francisco.

Only one PB-1 was built, but for the first time in a Boeing design, the wing used welded tubular truss steel spars and ribs. The original Model 80 had virtually an identical structure, although the later 80A wing used square-section aluminum tubing bolted into trusses instead of using welded round tubing. The same change was also made to the fuselage, which, on the 80, was made from welded steel tubing with some wire bracing, while on the 80A, it was changed to bolted square aluminum tubing aft of the cabin.

Powered by three Wasps, the Model 80 could reach speeds of up to 128 miles per hour and fly as high as 14,000 feet. Almost as soon as the first aircraft were in service, Boeing was already working hard on the next version, the 80A. Engines were again the differentiator. A more powerful successor to the Wasp, the 525-horsepower Hornet was supplied for the 80A, which could carry up to 18 passengers as a result. With so many passengers it became necessary to supply another crew member whose sole purpose was to look after the "payload." These first stewardesses were registered nurses and were provided with jump seats at the rear of the cabin. The aircrew were also far better off than their predecessors in having an enclosed cockpit.

New streamlining techniques were also applied to the redesigned 80A, which featured the new low-drag National Advisory Committee for Aeronautics (NACA) engine cowlings. The higher power of the Hornets also meant the necessary addition of two auxiliary fin and rudders to compensate for the higher asymmetric loads in the case of engine failure. The 10 80As were redesignated as 80A1s following the modification, which added weight. Fuel capacity was reduced as a result, in order to maintain the same takeoff weight. In another version of the aircraft, dubbed the 226, Boeing reversed this process and added more fuel. The 226 was built as a corporate transport for the Standard Oil Company and exchanged passengers for fuel. Capacity was increased to 658 gallons compared to 392 gallons in the 80A1s.

The Hornet also provided the power for Boeing's last airmail biplane, the Model 95. Twenty-five were built and delivered in 1929, most of which were operated either directly by BAT or its system operators. The 44-foot, 3-inch-span aircraft was notable for two main reasons. It was the first civil biplane to use the bolted square fuselage structure developed originally for the Model 83/89 fighters, and it was the first Boeing aircraft to be refueled in flight. This was accomplished by one aircraft that flew several nonstop transcontinental flights in 1929. The "Boeing Hornet Shuttle," as it was named, received fuel from an Army Douglas C-1 and a modified Boeing Model 40B-4 for the feat.

The company's first breakthrough into monoplane design came in May 1929 when it signed a contract with the Army to develop an experimental, all-metal monoplane fighter. In big picture terms, the leap to this type of design was already well under way by this time. Monoplanes had been well known since Bleriot's 1909 crossing of the English Channel, and Charles Lindbergh's nonstop crossing of the Atlantic in a Ryan-built monoplane had given further impetus to the move away from inefficient biplanes. To Boeing the design of the XP-9, as it was called, marked the beginning of a totally revolutionary design period. The company had virtually reached the peak of perfection when it came to military biplanes, and it was ready to take on the challenge of monoplanes.

In terms of overall design the XP-9 was not very radical. It was similar in configuration to the P-12/F4B and, in fact, used identical tail surfaces. The two-spar wing was mounted ahead of the pilot and appeared to rest on top of the fuselage where it was supported by two struts on either side. The most advanced feature was in the construction of the fuselage, which was of a semi-monocoque design. Metal formers supported a sheet dural skin from approximately halfway back down the length of the 25-foot, 1 3/4-inch-length fuselage. Forward of the aft-most strut the internal structure was of welded steel tubing.

The XP-9 was powered by a 600-horsepower Curtiss SV-15700 and could reach a maximum air speed of 213 miles per hour. Its handling qualities were very disappointing, however, particularly in directional stability, and a large vertical tail was added to improve this shortcoming. To Boeing's dismay, test pilots hated flying the aircraft, mainly because of bad visibility, and the Army did not order any more, despite the upgrade. Although the XP-9, therefore, went down in history as one of the worst aircraft created by Boeing, it nonetheless provided the all-important first venture into monoplane design and gave it experience that would more than make up for the lack of Army interest in the years to come.

The XP-9 was still in early design when Boeing hit on another more advanced application for its growing monoplane knowledge. The paramount need for speed was the prime driver in the development of new designs for the airmail service. The transition of monoplane technology seemed obvious to the company, which eagerly set about a new design called the Model 200. It was so enthusiastic about its new mail/cargo aircraft that it took the unprecedented step of naming it the Monomail.

The Monomail was a pivotal point in the history of Boeing aircraft. It was streamlined like no Boeing design before it. Its semi-monocoque metal fuselage was covered with smooth rather than corrugated skin. A NACA, low-drag ring cowl wrapped around the 575-horsepower Hornet engine, and the 59-foot, 1 1/2-inch-span wings were low-mounted and cantilevered, eliminating the need for bracing wires or support struts. Another first for this milestone aircraft was the retracting undercarriage. The main

The streamlined Model 200 Monomail represents a turning point in the Boeing design story. Everything from the cantilevered wing construction to the smooth skin was designed to make the Monomail go faster. It even had a retractable undercarriage, though by 1931, when this photograph was taken, the aircraft had been converted to the six-passenger Model 221 and was fitted with a fixed, streamlined landing gear. *Boeing*

gear legs retracted backward into the wing leaving half of each wheel exposed in the slipstream. The Monomail should have been a bestseller for Boeing, providing as it did a payload capacity of 220 cubic feet of cargo and mail and a range of 530 miles. However, it was too far ahead of its time in one critical aspect, that of propeller technology.

The concept of variable-pitch propellers was still in its infancy and, despite the streamlining and powerful Hornet engine, the fixed pitch blades simply could not cope. In initial tests the Monomail could barely taxi, let alone take off. Even after the blade pitch had been altered to provide some performance improvement at low levels, the Monomail made alarmingly long takeoff runs with even moderate payloads. At higher-altitude airports it was impossible to use the aircraft's full load potential. Boeing later tried developments of the original Monoplane with the new variable-pitch mechanism when it became available, but it was already too late. The Model 221, with a small 8-inch stretch and a cabin for six passengers, was the first development. This was then extended by another 27 inches to

make room for up to eight passengers, but no production models were ever built.

The Monomail had as much relevance for the future of Boeing's military aspirations as its civil hopes. Two twin-engined bomber aircraft, the Curtiss-powered GIV-1510C-powered 214 and the Hornet-powered 215 were built in quick succession. (See chapter 2) Other than different engine types, the two were identical and closely followed the aerodynamic and structural features pioneered by the Monomail. Despite its efforts to apply monoplane technology to large aircraft, the company did not neglect its smaller products. Boeing was not disheartened by its failure to win new fighter business with a proposed development of the XP-9 and pressed ahead with an entirely new monoplane design designated the Model 248. Design work began in mid-1931 and within three years led to the birth of the famous P-26 "Peashooter" fighter.

Although structurally similar to the Monomail and Model 218, the P-26 also borrowed features from

the Model 202/205 fighter. These began as company-sponsored projects in 1929 with the recognition that the days of the biplane fighter were numbered. The Model 202, or XP-15, was externally similar to the F4B/P-12 but with the lower wing deleted. Closer examination revealed an all-new metal fuselage similar to the XP-9 with semi-monocoque construction and dural skin. The tail was also covered with smooth rather than corrugated skin while the wings were constructed with dural built-up spars and ribs in place of the conventional wood. However, despite the XP-15's higher top speed of 190 miles per hour, the reduced wing area produced controllability problems. Neither the 202 nor its look-alike 205 sister ship (which was modified with fittings for a fighter-bomber role) won production contracts, but the structural lessons were plowed into the P-26.

At first glance the P-26 did not seem very advanced. It had a nonretractable undercarriage and stubby, wire-braced wings only 27 feet in span on the prototype. These

features were cleverly deliberate. Although the technology for retracting gear and cantilevered wings was available, Boeing recognized that the P-26 design was simple, sturdy, and less expensive to build and maintain. The wire bracing also negated the need for rigid struts, thus helping to reduce the weight of the structure. The fixed gear, although producing more drag, was lighter and simpler.

The Army tested the first aircraft, then designated the XP-936, and bought the three prototypes. Production orders were soon placed for 136 aircraft, of which the bulk, some 111 aircraft, was P-26As. These were later modified with flaps to reduce the landing speed, which was considered too excessive at the time. The P-26Bs and Cs were modified with flaps on the assembly line. Twelve export versions were also made, 11 for China and a single one for Spain. A squadron of P-26As was ultimately handed over to the Philippines, and one of these became one of the first Allied aircraft to shoot down a Japanese aircraft when targets in the Philippines were attacked in December 1941.

The famous P-26 combined the new streamlined benefits of the monoplanes with a few of the more durable features of the older biplane generation, such as the wire-braced wings, open cockpit, and fixed landing gear. This is the P-26 prototype, the XP-936, pictured at Boeing Field three days before its first flight on March 20, 1932. *Boeing*

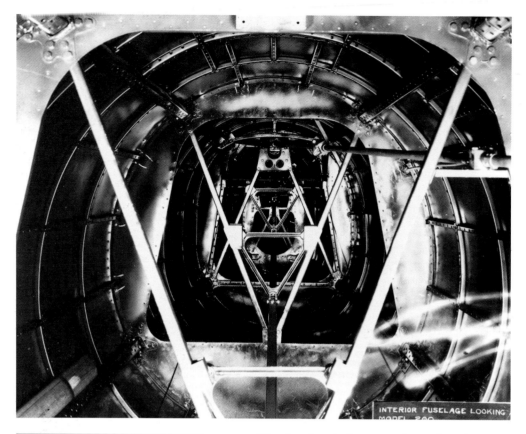

The Monomail was designed to be streamlined from the inside out. The internally stiffened semi-monocoque metal fuselage allowed the use of a low-drag, oval cross-section seen to good effect in this view when looking toward the tail. *Boeing*

A restored P-26A "Peashooter" in the 1935 markings of the 34th Pursuit Squadron at the Planes of Fame Museum in Chino, California. The peaked headrest behind the cockpit was increased to protect the pilot's head in case the aircraft flipped onto its back on landing or takeoff.

The aircraft cruised at 200 miles per hour but could "dash" at up to 234 miles per hour and was well liked by pilots who nicknamed it the "Peashooter." Powered by a 600-horsepower version of the ubiquitous Wasp, it was armed with two 30-caliber Browning machine guns, or one 30-caliber and one 50-caliber. The Peashooter marked the end of an era for Boeing which was already moving progressively into the design of larger aircraft. Apart from a brief attempt to reenter the market with an experimental Navy Fighter called the XF8B-1 (Boeing Model 400) in 1944, Boeing's next all new, independent fighter design, the Joint Strike Fighter, was still 60 years off in the future.

Problems with the 377's huge Pratt & Whitney R-4360 Double Wasp engines and hollow propeller blades plagued the aircraft for the first few years and even earned it the unfortunate nickname of the "best three-engined airliner on the North Atlantic." Here the first of eight Stratocruisers ordered by American Overseas Airlines, part of American, demonstrates level flight with number one and two engines off and propellers fully feathered. *Boeing*

2
Enter the Airliner

The late 1920s and early 1930s marked the start of a new phase from which Boeing never looked back. Up until this time design progress had been marked by a relatively slow trickle of advances from one model to another. The new era suddenly saw a cascade of technological innovations. The process that led to Boeing's commercial dominance by the last quarter of the twentieth century really began, somewhat ironically, when the company began work in 1930 on new bomber concepts under the model numbers 214 and 215.

The company-financed projects sought to capitalize on lessons learned from the Model 200 Monomail. Aerodynamic and structural concepts of the Model 200, such as low wings, retractable landing gear, and an all-metal structure were offered as a replacement for biplanes. The detailed design of what would become known as the B-9 bomber used new wind-tunnel data from tests conducted by the NACA at Langley Field, Virginia, in 1929. These proved that if engines were mounted on the leading edge of the wing rather than under them as on the latest trimotors, the drag was cut from 152 pounds to 25 pounds at 100 miles per hour.

Douglas and General Aviation (Fokker) were both competing for Army bomber business and were already well on the way with monoplane designs when Boeing started work on the B-9. Both Douglas, with the B-7, and Fokker, with

the XB-8, were at a disadvantage, however. The Douglas design was not structurally advanced, and the XB-8, although using engines with a thrust line centered on the airfoil, still had the traditional Fokker wooden wing and steel-tube fuselage. The Model 215 was almost identical to the 214 but used radial as opposed to inline, liquid-cooled engines and was completed ahead of its sister aircraft. The 215 flew first in April 1931 and displayed an instant likeness to the Monomail with its clean lines and cigar-shaped fuselage. It was larger than the Monomail with a span of 76 feet and a length of 56 feet and had almost double the wing area with 932 square feet.

The advances in its streamlined aerodynamic shape became obvious even before the Army began its tests. On a flight from Seattle to Dayton, Ohio, via Cheyenne and Chicago, the XB-9 (as it was designated) averaged 158 miles per hour. In tests at Wright Field's new Air Corps Materiel Division and test center, the B-9 proved itself revolutionary with a top speed of 188 miles per hour. At the time this was faster than U.S. Army "pursuit" aircraft such as the Keystone biplane that had a top speed of 121 miles per hour. The results led to an Army contract for the purchase of both the Model 214 and 215, which were now designated the Y1B-9 and YB-9, respectively. The 214 followed the 215 into the air

JUST A PLANE BOAT?
A 56-FT. YACHT OWNED BY DAVE DRIMMER, OF FORT LAUDERDALE, FLA., WAS CONVERTED FROM THE FUSELAGE OF HOWARD HUGHES' LUXURIOUS BOEING 307 STRATOLINER, "THE FLYING PENTHOUSE"-- THE BOAT'S CONTROLS ARE STILL LOCATED IN THE COCKPIT!

The
Seattle Museum of Flight's Model 247D purrs into land like a time warp at Boeing Field more than 60 years after it left the factory to begin service with United Airlines.

Although
United was the major customer for the 247, it also killed it in the long run. The airline's pilots forced Boeing to scale down the aircraft to enable it to use Wasp engines instead of the Hornet as planned, thus hopelessly compromising the design. It also blocked out production for more than a year, forcing other airlines to go to Douglas, which came up with the winning DC-2 and DC-3 as a result.

in November 1931 and was eventually converted to use the same Curtiss GIV-1570 engine.

Encouraged by the early test results and the Army's contract, Boeing confidently expected a big production order. To its shock, the contract went to the Glenn L. Martin Company, which upstaged Boeing with an extremely similar but more advanced design called the XB-907. The twin-engined bomber was ordered into production as the B-10 and B-12, seemingly leaving Boeing out in the cold.

But all was not lost. The B-9 development had pioneered new technology such as control surface trim tabs and servo tabs to reduce pilot forces resulting from the increase in size and speed. With a gross weight of 13,608 pounds, the B-9 was Boeing's biggest aircraft yet. It also led to the development of techniques to counteract the relatively unknown phenomenon of "flutter," which began to appear as speeds increased. This was a condition in which the aerodynamic forces acting on the control surfaces would be slightly uneven, causing it to begin vibrating, or "fluttering." The flutter could quickly get out control, bending and twisting the entire wing before causing the control surface—and sometimes the wing itself—to fail.

The cure was a simple "mass balance" about the hinge line of the control surface. The B-9 had tail flutter that was made worse by the torsional flexibility of the long fuselage. The condition was cured by the addition of weight to balance it around the hinge line. Due to the large forces acting on the rudder, servo tabs were also added, becoming the first to be installed on any U.S.-built aircraft. On the Model 214, the tab was a small projection aft of the main rudder, whereas on the 215 it was a tall, narrow strip running along the entire rudder trailing edge.

MODEL 247

Boeing was determined not to waste the potential of the B-9. An opportunity to build on its technology soon emerged in the form of an airliner project—the Model 247. United Airlines group, part of the huge United Aircraft and Transport Corporation, which included Boeing, was being challenged in 1931 by a new airline called Transcontinental & Western Air. TWA was the former TAT "Lindbergh Line" and operated Ford Trimotors and Fokker F-32s that completely outclassed United's Model 80 fleet. United asked its sister company to come up with a design to meet the TWA challenge.

Boeing had studied new airliner concepts since 1929 and had come up with a high-wing monoplane trimotor powered by the new 575-horsepower P&W Hornet engine as well as an all-metal biplane design similar to the Model 80. The pilot community vetoed both designs, however, particularly because the Hornet was considered a little too large for commercial use and pilots were used to handling the reliable 525-horsepower Wasp engine. United, however, wanted an aircraft as least as big as the 18-passenger Model 80. Boeing was torn between the two but was more concerned about speed, weight, single-engine performance, and above all, cost.

With the experience of the B-9 so fresh on everyone's memory, the obvious solution became a twin-engined airliner based on the bomber configuration. The problem of what engine and propeller to use still hung over the decision makers when preliminary design began in September 1931. The close tie-up with P&W prevented Boeing from investigating a new engine then in development by Wright. The Wright 1820 engine was ultimately very successful, powering both the B-17 and a twin called the DC-1 from a new challenger, the Douglas Aircraft Company. Boeing chose not to wait for the thorough testing of either the Wright engine or a more powerful P&W engine then under development and went ahead with the design of the 247 based on the Wasp.

The decision was crucial. It gained Boeing a short-term advantage but ultimately doomed the 247 to a short production life and limited career. Another mistake was the decision to use fixed pitch propellers whose limitations had been painfully obvious on the Monomail. The advantage of a controllable pitch propeller was that the blade angle could be adjusted to suit different phases of flight. It would be set at a "fine" pitch, or almost edge on the airflow, for takeoff when the air was most dense, allowing use of maximum engine rpm. As the aircraft climbed into thinner air and accelerated, the pitch was increased, or coarsened, to prevent the engine from overspeeding.

As with the engine choice, Boeing opted for the fixed prop option for reasons of simplicity, cost, and expediency. Hamilton Standard, the propeller manufacturer that was a part of United Aircraft along with Boeing, had developed a variable-pitch blade as early as 1929, but by 1933 when the 247 was in final design, only a two-bladed prop had been tested with this adaptation. The proximity of the 247's engines to the fuselage prohibited the use of a two-blade prop, and Boeing was forced to wait for Hamilton Standard to adapt the pitch change mechanism to the three-bladed prop selected for the 247. Controllable propellers were first used on the DC-1, and by the time they

The Model 247 was the first low-wing, twin-engined U.S. airliner. The streamlined, semi-monocoque fuselage and cantilevered wing borrowed heavily from the Monomail and B-9 bomber, but the two main wing spars ran awkwardly right through the cabin, as pictured here.
Boeing

The ergonomics of the 247 cockpit, were in some ways, a step backwards from the Model 80A. Engine instruments, for example, were located only on the copilot's side (right), while the basic flight instruments were located centrally.

were installed and certificated on the 247D version in October 1934, Boeing had already lost the marketing initiative to Douglas.

Another factor that swung in favor of Douglas was the allocation of the first 60 247s to United. Other carriers like TWA were unable to secure early positions for 247 deliveries, so they were forced to negotiate with other manufacturers, particularly Douglas, which subsequently worked closely with TWA on the design of the DC-1. The development time lag benefited the DC-1 and its production successors the DC-2 and DC-3, which were able to take advantage of new advances in engine technology and aerodynamics. The newer engines were also easier to cool, which allowed the use of the long NACA engine cowl. This reduced drag even more than the short-ring Townend

cowl named after its British inventor and used on the 247. The full NACA cowlings were eventually used on the 247D and retrofitted on earlier production aircraft. The D model also had metal-covered tail control surfaces instead of the original fabric, variable-pitch props and a new windshield that sloped upward and aft.

Despite its shortcomings, the 247 was nothing less than revolutionary. It was the first low-wing, multi-engine U.S. transport and was up to 70 miles per hour faster than any of its immediate competitors. One aircraft originally ordered by United was flown by Col. Roscoe Turner and Clyde Pangborn in the 1934 MacRobertson air race from England to Australia. The fast aircraft finished second in the transport division and placed third in overall speed. The 247 crossed the United States in less than 20 hours and was the first twin monoplane able to climb with a full load after the failure of either engine in flight. Other advances included a rudimentary automatic pilot and de-icing equipment.

The 247s established a good safety record and were efficient money makers for the few carriers under the United banner that operated them. But the decision not to use Hornet engines and to scale the 247 down virtually doomed it from the drawing board. Its chief accomplishment was to spur Douglas and Lockheed to more modern airliner configurations.

MODEL 307 STRATOLINER

The sudden loss of the airline business to Douglas was a bitter pill for Boeing to swallow, particularly since the 247 had been the trend setter. The stagnant order book in 1934 also coincided with the passing of a new law that had dramatic repercussions for Boeing. The Air Mail Act ordered that airline companies divorce themselves completely from aircraft manufacturers, thus forcing United Aircraft and Air Transport to split into three independent companies. Out of the maelstrom emerged United Airlines, United Aircraft Corporation, and the Boeing Airplane Company, which also included Stearman Aircraft in Wichita, Kansas.

The enforced breakup of the company not only deprived it of a steadfast partner and customer, it also led to the resignation of an embittered William E. Boeing, who accused the administration of President Franklin Roosevelt of acting unfairly. To make matters worse for an increasingly beleaguered Boeing, it soon discovered that its old partner United had put together a group of airlines to underwrite the development of a new Douglas airliner! The DC-4E, as the project was called, was supported by TWA, Eastern, Pan Am, and American and included the provision that none would buy a new airliner of more than 50,000 pounds gross weight before giving Douglas first pass. Pressure was also mounting from Lockheed, which in 1935 won an Army contract to build and test a pressurized fuselage for the Model 10 Electra. The XC-35 was not tested until 1937, but it offered Lockheed a competitive edge nonetheless.

Faced with these developments, Boeing knew it had to come up with an attractive, new design, and quickly, if it wanted to stay in the airliner business. Salvation came in the form of a study aircraft (Model 300) derived from the XB-17 (Model 299) (see chapter 3). Created largely by chief engineer Ed Wells, the design used the wings,

engines, and undercarriage of the B-17C bomber but was adapted with a completely circular, fully pressurized fuselage. The specification for what was to become the Model 307 was drawn up by December 1935, and Boeing went out to sell the concept to airlines.

Through 1936 Boeing canvassed Pan Am and TWA, which both declared high interest in the unusual concept of an airliner that could fly above the weather. As air travel matured in the early 1930s, the growing need for pressurization was increasingly obvious. On transcontinental routes involving flights across the Rockies, the stewardesses patrolled the cabin with oxygen bottles, offering distressed passengers a whiff from the mask. The airlines discovered that pilots needed oxygen above 8,000 feet to stay alert and that without oxygen night blindness could occur at 12,000 feet. To drive home the new high-altitude concept, Boeing called its new aircraft the Stratoliner, becoming only the third company aircraft, after the Monomail and Flying Fortress, to be formally named.

By 1937 Pan Am and TWA were ready to sign but were still concerned about their obligation to Douglas over what was by now the late and overbudget DC-4E. Boeing presented the final specifications to both airlines, showing projected gross weight for the 307 to be just 42,000 pounds, a full 8,000 pounds below the DC-4E cutoff weight. Satisfied with this, Pan American Airways ordered four and TWA ordered six. The capabilities of the aircraft attracted the tycoon Howard Hughes, who wanted to use

The most famous 247D, now preserved at the Smithsonian's National Air and Space Museum in Washington, D.C., was flown in the 1934 MacRobertson air race from England to Australia by Col. Roscoe Turner and Clyde Pangborn. Ironically, it was forced into second place in the transport category by its nemesis, the DC-2.

the 307 to make an attempt on his own recently set round-the-world record.

According to some sources, Hughes was told he would have to wait until TWA had received its six aircraft before he could get one of the $315,000 307s. Frustrated with this, the unpredictable Hughes immediately went out and bought a controlling interest in the financially troubled airline, diverting the first of the fleet for his own use and reducing the TWA purchase to five! Other accounts portray Hughes' involvement as a way of helping TWA president Jack Frye overrule the majority stockholder, John Hertz, who was opposed to expenditure on the new aircraft. Hertz later went on to found the rental car company that still bears his name.

The first 307 flew on December 31, 1938, and flight tests progressed well until disaster struck on March 18, 1939. The 307 was on a demonstration flight for the Netherlands flag carrier, KLM, when one engine was shut down at 10,000 feet to show handling characteristics at low air speed. The aircraft suddenly stalled, and the rudder locked into position at the limit of its travel, flipping the 307 onto its back and into an inverted spin. Witnesses said the crew managed to stop the spin and began to pull the aircraft out of the dive by around 3,000 feet, but the forces were too much for the airframe, and the wings failed. Wreckage fell to the ground near Mount Rainier, and all aboard were killed.

The 307 had been proving difficult to sell, and the crash put the final nail in the coffin for Boeing's marketers. Yet the improvements that were developed for the surviving 307s made them extremely safe and stable and had a profound effect on the outcome of later models of the B-17. The most obvious changes included a new rudder and the addition of a large dorsal fin to improve lateral control, while a slotted leading edge was developed to improve stall resistance at high angles of attack. The bigger vertical tail was to become a hallmark of all subsequent Boeing designs, just as small tails had been a distinguishing—and limiting—feature of all its aircraft up to this point.

The biggest distinction of the 307, however, remained its unique pressurization system. At altitudes between 8,000 feet and 14,700 feet, the 33 passengers housed in the Pullman-like luxury of the circular fuselage experienced pressure conditions that remained the equivalent of 8,000 feet. At 16,000 feet the pressure altitude was 9,000 feet; at 18,000 feet it was 10,600 feet; and at 20,000

feet it was 12,300 feet. This meant that between 14,700 feet and 20,000 feet, the pressure inside the cabin exceeded the outside atmospheric pressure by 2.5 pounds per square inch. This was less than half the 6-pounds-per square-inch difference for which the fuselage was designed.

Air was sucked into the system through intakes on the leading edge of the wing. It passed through a water separator to remove rain and into a supercharger, which pressurized the air. It then passed through a thermostatically controlled steam-heating unit in the engine nacelle before going through a Boeing-developed automatic flow control valve into the cabin via a distribution valve. After circulating through the cabin, the air passed through vents in the floor to an automatic outlet control valve that controlled the atmospheric pressure in the cabin. A relief valve in the rear of the cabin discharged any excess pressure if any of the main valves malfunctioned.

The supercharger was one of the most critical technical advances of the entire system. As well as assisting in pressurization, it was developed to help the 900-horsepower Wright Cyclone engines produce sufficient power at the much higher operating altitudes of the 307. As atmospheric pressure and density at 20,000 feet is less than half that at sea level, piston engines would literally run out of

OPPOSITE
Thanks to the innovation of pressurization, the 307 was able to cruise at altitudes up to 26,200 feet—or closer to the stratosphere than ever before and above much of the rougher weather for the first time. To emphasize this high-flying capability, Boeing dubbed it the "Stratoliner," kicking off a long line of strato-related products. *Boeing*

The flight engineer controlled cabin pressurization via the panel outlined in white. The pressure was controlled by an outlet control valve, the switch for which is located at the top left-hand corner of the panel. *Boeing*

Restoration work on this ex-Pan American Airways PAA-307 at Boeing reveals the aft-pressure bulkhead. This sealed the aft end of the cabin pressure vessel, which was totally circular as a result. The basic structure remains largely unchanged on current airliners even to this day.

A General Electric-produced supercharger increased the air pressure as it was fed from the wing's leading edge to a thermostatically controlled steam-heating unit. Metallurgical skills developed for the supercharger, seen here on the similar nacelle of a B-17G, led directly to the selection of GE as first choice to produce an American version of the British-developed Whittle jet engine.

breath. Engine designers in France, England, and the United States developed methods of "supercharging" the air being pumped into the engine to compensate for this, but by the late 1930s only General Electric in the United States had persisted with the concept of a supercharger driven by the exhaust gases of the engine itself.

The problem with this approach lay in the development of metal that could withstand the white-hot temperatures of the exhaust. Breakthroughs in GE's metallurgical skills allowed the company to make a turbine wheel that would survive this savagely hot environment and produce a workable design. The turbine was spun at speeds up to 50,000 rpms on the same shaft as a centrifugal blower. Air ducted into the engine from a ram intake was then compressed up to three times the pressure of the thin upper atmosphere. This was fed to the downgoing pistons, which drew in a much heavier weight of air as a result. This meant a correspondingly greater weight of oxygen, which makes up about 21 percent of the atmosphere. The quantity of oxygen drawn into the cylinder determined the amount of fuel that could be burned, and hence the power that could be produced.

The development of the supercharger (or turbosupercharger as it was sometimes called) to help pressurize and power the 307 also boosted the parallel application of this technology on the B-17. The modification transformed the performance of the bomber, helping it gain new respectability after the 1935 crash (see chapter 3), and guaranteed large production orders with the growing threat of war. Importantly, GE's experience with superchargers led to its selection in 1941 as the company to bring the British-developed Whittle jet engine to the United States.

Building the first pressurized airliner also taught Boeing new tricks that would later come to be essential when designing virtually every product from the B-29 onwards. Manufacturing and quality control techniques were upgraded to deal with the new technology. Skin joints of the 307 were covered with a fabric tape that sealed up holes when the rivets were punched through. To confirm that the seal was solid, the joints were lathered with soap suds, and the cabin would be pressurized. If any air bubbles came up, the affected area was reriveted. Boeing also had to develop its own pressure chamber to test the components of the system such as the pressure regulator.

Pan American Airways' (PAA) three aircraft entered service on the Latin American routes out of the carrier's

Miami base while TWA began using its aircraft on heavily publicized "over the weather" coast-to-coast services via Chicago, Kansas City, Albuquerque, and Los Angeles. The small fleet brought a short-lived period of unaccustomed luxury and comfort to the air travelers of the day. The 12-foot-wide cabin allowed unprecedented room to stand up and even walk around. The interiors were soundproofed and air-conditioned with individual lights and ash trays at each seat. The standard interior was made up of four six-passenger compartments along the right side of the cabin, opposite which were nine individual reclining chairs along the left side of the main aisleway. At night the compartments were converted into 16 upper and lower sleeping berths. Forward of the main cabin was a large dressing room for men, complete with the then novel accessory of an electric shaver. At the left rear was a full-size galley while the right rear was allocated for a woman's "charm room."

The 307's glory days did not last long, however, as the onset of war saw TWA's fleet quickly pressed into service with the Army Air Transport Command. Designated as C-75s, they were used to train pilots in long-range four-engined operations and trailblazed Air Transport

The ravages of time are evident on the rotting fabric-covered ailerons and fading paintwork of this ex-PAA aircraft as it bides its time at the Pima County Air Museum in Arizona in 1989. By 1998 the 307 was in the advanced stages of restoration in the place of its creation almost 60 years earlier.

Command's transatlantic routes. By the end of their service days, the five C-75s had made around 3,000 oceanic flights and logged more than 45,000 hours.

In 1944 they were returned to Boeing to be reworked into what amounted to an almost-new aircraft. Redesignated the SA-307B-1 (TWA's aircraft were originally SA-307Bs, and PAA's were S-307s), the five were fitted with the wings, nacelles, and larger horizontal tails of the B-17G. The Wright Cyclone engines were replaced by the 1,200-horsepower GR-1829-G666 version, providing an increase of more than 100 horsepower per engine. The electrical system was completely revised to the latest standards adopted for the B-29, and the pressurization system was removed. The extra engine power and deletion of the heavy pressurization system allowed gross takeoff weight to be increased to 45,000 pounds and passenger loads to grow to 38.

For the remainder of their TWA careers the 307B-1s soldiered on, flying low-level domestic routes until they were sold to French carrier Aigle Azur in 1951. Three of the old war-horses were eventually based out of Saigon during the Vietnam War and, for a while, were the only civil aircraft allowed to fly to the North Vietnamese capital, Hanoi. None of the three survived the war, two were written off in accidents while a third was shot down mistakenly by a U.S. fighter. By the late 1990s only two of the planes survived, one of which was back in the safe hands of former Boeing 307 workers and kept in Seattle's Museum of Flight. The other, rather bizarrely, survives in the shape of a luxurious houseboat in Florida, where it was saved from scrap and converted after being damaged by a hurricane. Ironically, this aircraft was the former personal aircraft of Howard Hughes.

MODEL 314 CLIPPER

Although the breakup of the large United group forced Boeing into some tough reorganization, it had some indirect benefits, including the faster promotion of younger engineers with bright ideas. One of these was Wellwood Beall, a graduate of the Guggenheim School of Aeronautics at New York University and chief engineering instructor at the Boeing School of Aeronautics in Oakland.

The mighty Model 314 is credited as the brainchild of Beall, who at the time was making his way back to the United States from China, where he had been selling pursuit aircraft. Beall heard rumors that Pan American was

OPPOSITE
With a standard maximum takeoff weight of around 42,000 pounds, the 307 could climb at 1,200 feet per minute on all four engines or at 600 feet per minute on three. Even with just two operating, it could still manage more than 100 feet per minute. Ceiling with three engines and a full load was an impressive 18,000 feet.

One remarkable 307 survivor is now used as a houseboat in Florida. The aircraft, an SB-307B, was acquired by Howard Hughes in 1938 for an attempt on his own flight round-the-world record set earlier that year in a Lockheed Model 14. The outbreak of World War II thwarted the record attempt, and the aircraft became an executive transport known as the "Flying Penthouse." After passing through the hands of several owners, it was badly damaged by a storm in 1964 at the Fort Lauderdale-Hollywood International Airport. The remains were bought for $100 by Ken London, who converted it into a houseboat. The boat has been owned by Dave Drimmer since 1981.

considering a westward extension of its transpacific routes to China and hatched plans for a huge flying boat that might do the job. Sure enough, PAA again provided the stimulus by inviting proposals from seven manufacturers for a long-range flying boat and even added the incentive of a $50,000 bonus to the winner.

Strangely, Boeing emerged as the only bidder; neither Martin, which built PAA's M-130 China Clipper flying boats, nor Sikorsky, the maker of the famous S-40 and S-42 aircraft, even competed. Talks between Boeing and PAA started in earnest in 1935, but the model number 307 was not adopted until negotiations over a firm configuration had taken place in early 1936. Eventually, on July 21, 1936, PAA signed a $4.8 million contract for six aircraft plus six options. Each of the $512,000 Model 314s was designated a "Clipper" at PAA's request to conform with its other fleets.

As it did with the Model 307, which was actually started and completed after the flying boat, Boeing was able to take advantage of the newly developed wing and nacelles of a bomber to provide a jump-start on the program. In this case Beall used the massive wing of the XB-15, which was in the final stages of construction at the time (see chapter 3). The wings were added to the bulbous

fuselage of the flying boat, giving a huge wingspan of 152 feet, some 3 feet wider than the XB-15 and 11 feet greater than even the enormous B-29, which was to follow four years later. Unlike most large flying boats of its day, the Model 314 did not have wing tip floats. Instead, stability was provided by large sponsons, or hydro-stabilizers, which were also used to hold fuel. Added to the enormous tanks of the deep wing, the fuel capacity was eventually increased with later modifications by 1,200 U.S. gallons to a total of 5,408 U.S. gallons. The initial fuel capacity was enough for a normal cruising range of 3,685 miles, although at maximum weight the 314 was capable of cruising up to 4,900 miles. The heavier 314A, complete with extra fuel capacity, could manage 5,200-mile routes—an incredible feat for its day.

In keeping with the most recent engine developments, Boeing substituted the XB-15's 850-horsepower P&W 1830 Twin Wasps for more powerful 1,500-horsepower Wright GR-2600 Double Cyclones. These were also ultimately superseded on the 314A by 1,600-horsepower Wright Cyclone 709C-14AC1 double-row, 14-cylinder radials. The deep wing, built like the XB-15 and 307 wing, was roomy enough for a companionway that the crew could use to access the engines during the flight.

Early tests showed the Model 314 urgently needed more tail surfaces, and several configurations were tried out on the prototype before the final shape, shown here, was adopted. These huge flying boats were the last production aircraft built at Boeing's Plant 1, and because of their sheer size, final assembly took place on the old launching ramp outside. *Boeing*

The 314 shared many features with the XB-15 bomber, including this spacious "flight deck," as it was christened. The pilot and copilot, radio officer, flight engineer, and navigator are all visible in this photograph. The sixth crew member was the aircraft commander. *Boeing*

The most unusual aspects of the giant flying boat were found within the hull. This was by now the standard semi-monocoque structure but was divided up into 11 sections by truss-type bulkheads and split lengthwise into two decks. The bulkheads were extended below the lower deck floor to the flush-riveted bottom skin of the hull to create a series of watertight compartments. The upper deck contained the "control cabin," or flight deck, aft of which were the main cargo, mail, and baggage holds. Additional space for cargo was also provided in the bow of the hull for a total capacity of around 5 tons. The passenger deck below was divided into 9 sections, including a lounge seating 12, 6 separate passenger compartments, and a specially furnished deluxe compartment that originated as a honeymoon suite. A spiral staircase connected the two decks. The complex hull also contained a galley as well as separate bathrooms for men and women. These were the first flushable toilets developed for an airliner and were part of the many advances that made the Clippers the most luxurious mode of transport when they finally entered service in 1939. Initial flights were restricted to transatlantic airmail duties from late May 1939, but passenger services began on June 28 that year. In most configurations the 314 was operated by a crew of 11, including 2 stewards, and accommodated up to 68 day passengers or 36 in the sleeper layout. In some aircraft the day load was increased to 70 and the sleeper load to 40 while crew numbers were cut to 10.

The first 314s were originally due to be handed over to PAA in early 1938, but problems plagued the development. These mainly concerned directional control problems both in the air and on the water during takeoff and taxiing. These had arisen during initial sea trials and the first flight in June 1938. The dihedral of the hydro-stabilizers was reduced to help cure the 314's marked tendency to dip a wing tip in the water when caught by the wind during a turn. The biggest problem was insufficient rudder authority in the air. The cumbersome 314 required full rudder and differential power to execute even the most moderate turn. As a result, the single fin was replaced by two fins mounted at the end of the horizontal tail. This also proved inadequate during trials, and the original fin was added back to the assembly to create a triple-tail arrangement similar to the Lockheed Constellation.

Like the 307s, the 314s were quickly overtaken by the tide of war. The crew of one aircraft, *Pacific Clipper*, caught in New Zealand by the outbreak of hostilities in Asia in

December 1941, elected to fly back to the United States "the long way round" the world rather than attempt a flight back through what was then a war zone. The *Pacific Clipper* flew back home via Australia, India, the Middle East, Central Africa, the South Atlantic, and South America, alighting in New York harbor on January 6, 1942, after almost circumnavigating the globe on its 34,500 mile journey.

Under pressure from President Roosevelt, PAA sold three 314As to British Overseas Airways Corporation (BOAC) before the United States entered the war itself. After December 1941 the remaining nine PAA aircraft (all now modified as 314As with extra fuel and higher power engines) were drafted into service for the U.S. Army and Navy. The Army's Transport Command designated four of the flying boats as C-98s, while the balance were lent back to PAA for its own use but under Navy control. These aircraft were operated by PAA crews under contract to the Navy but carried their original civil registrations painted against a Navy sea-gray camouflage. The three BOAC-operated aircraft flew more than 4.25 million miles, crossed the Atlantic 596 times, and carried slightly more than 40,000 passengers without loss. By the end of the war, the other nine aircraft had similarly amassed more than 8 million miles on more than 3,600 ocean crossings.

The prewar glory days of the flying boat era did not return with the end of hostilities. Bigger, faster, more reliable landplanes were available to airlines, and a fully functioning airways system, complete with concrete runways, was

Despite many perilous trips made during World War II, the only serious accident befell this 314, *Yankee Clipper*. The aircraft crashed into the Tagus River near Lisbon, Portugal, in February 1942, killing 24 of the 39 aboard. The aircraft's fourth officer, John Burns, saved one of the passengers, a singer named Jane Froman, and the two were later married. Clippers were otherwise sturdy and reliable and were frequently used by President Franklin Roosevelt and British Prime Minister Winston Churchill. *Boeing*

available to support them. As a result, there was no demand from the major carriers for the surviving 314As, which were either scrapped or used by charter operators in the last few years of their careers. The last survivor, the former BOAC aircraft *Bristol,* was scrapped after being raised from the bottom of Baltimore Harbor, where it sank in a violent storm.

Although the 314 was not the runaway success Boeing had hoped for, it taught the company valuable lessons on big aircraft design, manufacture, and development. In general, however, the 314 was something of a technical cul-de-sac. Some hull features of the 314, but not the hydro-stabilizers, were used on the abortive XPBB-1 long-range Naval patrol bomber. The bomber (Model 344) used the baseline B-29 wing and had a span of almost 140 feet. Unusually, it was designed to fly with only two Wright R-3350 engines, making it the largest twin-engined aircraft ever built up until its first flight in July 1942. The Sea Ranger, as Boeing called it, was overtaken by the changing strategic situation, and an initial production order for 57 was canceled. The "Lone Ranger," as the aircraft was thereafter unofficially called, marked the end of Boeing's association with big seaplanes.

MODEL 377 STRATOCRUISER

Boeing's largest and last piston-engined transport was the Model 377 Stratocruiser, a commercial derivative of the military C-97. This rugged transport, developed as the Model 367, was in turn based on the B-29 bomber. The Model 367 followed the increasingly successful "building block" formula developed for the Model 307 Stratocruiser in which the wings, tails, nacelles, and undercarriage of the B-17 were used as the basis for the next growth step.

Although priority was given to bomber development and production, three prototypes were ordered in January 1942 under contract from the Air Service Technical Command of the Army Air Force. The first aircraft was designated the XC-97 and made its maiden flight on November 9, 1944. Two months later the huge potential of the frankly cumbersome-looking aircraft was amply demonstrated when the first prototype sped across the United States from Seattle to Washington, D.C., in 6 hours and 3 minutes. The aircraft was carrying 20,000 pounds of payload and covered the 3,323 miles at an average speed of 383 miles per hour, setting a new speed record for an air transport category aircraft.

A B-47 noses up to the flying boom dangling behind a KC-97 refueling tanker. In all, 890 military C/KC-97 were built, of which 816 were ordered specifically as tankers. The growth of jets like the B-47 also spelled the end of the KC-97s, which were too slow to be effective. Note the slight nose-down attitude of the tanker as it fights for speed during the transfer. *Boeing*

technique for the Stratocruiser was often the unorthodox nose-wheel-first method, particularly if the runway was short or braking action poor. Here a former USAF C-97G Stratofreighter, converted into a freighter for Agro Air of the Dominican Republic, nears touchdown at Miami International in March 1988. Note the electrically operated flaps, which increase wing area by 19 percent when fully extended.

Key to this successful demonstration was its ability to cruise at 30,000 feet and take advantage of jet stream tailwinds. Following in the footsteps of the 307 and the B-29, the XC-97 was pressurized to allow it to operate above the weather. Unlike the B-29, however, in which only the forward crew compartment was pressurized, the XC-97 was pressurized throughout its entire length with the exception of storage areas in the tail. To cope with the structural loads of pressurization on this scale and yet accommodate the freighter's larger capacity, Boeing designers adapted a "double-bubble" fuselage cross-section first used by Curtiss on the C-46. As a result, the fuselage was made up of two intersecting circular sections and essentially resembled an inverted figure eight. Given the stresses of cabin pressurization, the engineers decided it was easier to build one fuselage on top of another than encompass the same 3,000-cubic-foot cargo volume in a single ellipse.

The resulting shape had twice the volume of the B-29, and was 12 feet longer. The lower section also retained the same cross-sectional diameter of the B-29 but the upper lobe was significantly wider with a diameter of 11 feet. The 78-foot-long main cabin could accommodate up to 134 troops, three one-and-a-half-ton trucks, or even two light tanks. These could be driven up a ramp into the fuselage through clamshell doors built into the sloping belly area in the rear fuselage. An electrically powered cargo hoist ran the entire length of the fuselage along a rail mounted in the roof of the cabin. This could be used to pick up loads from the trucks or from the ground through the loading doors.

Production of 10 test models, designated YC-97s, was authorized in July 1945, beginning an 11-year run that would turn out 835 military aircraft. The true value of the bulbous aircraft, however, was as an airborne tanker, and of the total around 800 were either built from scratch or converted to KC-97 tanker variants. Of all the submodels the most prolific was the KC-97G, of which 592 were built. This was built as a tanker but could be easily adapted to a freighter role without the need to remove the inflight refueling tanks from the main cabin. Production ended in 1956 when the new KC-135A Stratotanker began replacing it on the Renton line.

One of the early aircraft, the 10th and last service test C-97, provided the blueprint for the first Stratocruiser. The sole YC-97B was fitted out as a VIP personnel transport with airline-like seating for 80, separate men's and women's dressing rooms, and a lounge in the lower deck behind the wings. Boeing's newly elected

president William Allen saw the C-97, and in particular the example set by the YC-97B, as the company's best chance of re-entering the postwar airline market. Like all the big aircraft manufacturers, Boeing faced an uncertain future as the inevitable postwar recession began to bite. Military orders tumbled, and jobs were cut, so Boeing began looking at a strictly commercial variant to fill the gap—the Model 377 Stratocruiser.

Douglas and Lockheed were better prepared for the fray as both had already developed reliable and well-liked transports for the Army Air Force. Douglas was selling its DC-4 to airlines by war's end and working furiously on a pressurized 50-seater derivative dubbed the DC-6. Lockheed made the brave decision to keep its C-69 Constellation line open, despite the cancellation of its military contracts. All aircraft, complete or incomplete, were converted to the civil 049 configuration, and surplus C-69s were bought back from the Army and refurbished. By November 1945 Lockheed announced orders for up to 89 049s, most of which were from U.S. airlines. Spurred on by a request from Eastern Airlines, as well as news of the DC-6 and Boeing's launch of the 377, Lockheed began work in May 1946 on newer versions called the 649 and 749. The race was on.

Boeing's launch of the 377 was nothing short of an act of faith. As almost one of his first moves after becoming president in September 1945, Allen authorized the production of 50 Stratocruisers before a single aircraft had been sold. It was, in effect, buying the aircraft itself. At an estimated price of $1.5 million per copy this was an extremely risky move but one that Allen was totally committed to. However, as Boeing sales teams fanned out to sell the expensive airliner, they had at least one ace to play. The record-breaking transcontinental run of the prototype XC-97 in January had at least proved the potential of the Stratocruiser, which was designed from the outset to use even more powerful P&W R-4360 Double Wasp engines.

Once again Pan American came to Boeing's help. On November 28, 1945, it ordered 20 Stratocruisers in a contract valued at $24.5 million, a record at the time for a commercial airliner deal. Other orders slowly trickled in but not as many as Boeing hoped. Four were ordered by the Danish, Norwegian, and Swedish airlines, which were in the process of combining to form what was to become Scandinavian Airline System (SAS). American Overseas Airlines, the international arm of American Airlines, ordered 8 and Northwest signed for 10. BOAC also ordered 6 but went on to operate a fleet of 17, as it bought

A flight engineer's view of the daunting engine and systems controls of the KC-97. Above and behind the pilots' positions is the equally elaborate circuit-breaker panel.

used Stratocruisers from other operators. In all just 55 were built, excluding the 377 prototype, and were delivered between February 1949 and March 1950.

Engine problems plagued the Stratocruiser from the start and prevailed to the extent that it was infamously called "the best three-engined transatlantic airliner." The enormous R-4360 "wasp major" was perhaps the ultimate piston engine and was the largest, most powerful, and last air-cooled radial engine designed and produced by P&W. In all, between 1944 and 1955, P&W produced 18,679 of these monster engines, which had the capacity to generate up to 4,300 horsepower at 2,700 rpm. Key to its power and complexity was the design of its four-row, semi-staggered spiral cylinder arrangement. With this design, P&W cunningly packed 28 cylinders with a displacement of

4,360 cubic inches behind the 16-foot, 7-inch-diameter Hamilton-Standard propellers. The major problem was that the engine, and particularly the back row of cylinders, would begin to run at too high a temperature, leading to total engine failure.

The engine successfully powered a wide variety of other aircraft including Northrop's B-35 Flying Wing, the Douglas C-74 and C-124 Globemaster, and even Howard Hughes' giant "Spruce Goose" flying boat. However, it had proved its ability to run continuously without problems on another Boeing product, the B-50. In one case a B-50 named *Lucky Lady II* had become the first aircraft to fly nonstop around the world when it circumnavigated the globe in early 1949. The feat was accomplished (with airborne refueling) in 94 hours, 1 minute, during which each

of its four "Wasp Major" engines had run continuously and without fault for almost four straight days of flying. Faced with this evidence, Boeing and PAA studied the problem and revised the cowling design to funnel more cooling air around the back end of the engine. Other problems were also caused by the failure of new hollow steel blades. Balance weights inside the tips worked loose and caused the blades to vibrate so violently that they would, in the worst cases, rip the entire engine from its mounting. This was the cause attributed to at least two fatal Stratocruiser accidents. The solution was a return to more conventional solid blades.

The problems with the sophisticated engines in many ways encapsulated those of the aircraft itself. The Stratocruiser was, along with aircraft such as the DC-7C and

L-1649A, one of the ultimate piston-engined airliners. Yet even as they were handed over to their new owners, these magnificent flying machines were already obsolete. The age of the piston was over, and the age of the jet had already begun. Boeing itself had recognized this and was working on new jet-powered derivatives of the 367. The winning version was the 80th configuration, simply called the 367-80, which was ultimately to become the 707 and KC-135 (see chapter 4).

The Stratocruiser, and to a lesser extent the C-97, had one more bizarre contribution to make. The second ex-PAA aircraft was bought by California-based Aero Space Lines Corporation for use in transporting large space rocket subassemblies from factories on the west coast to Florida. Using a parallel fuselage section from another scrapped Stratocruiser, the

The glasshouse feel of the flight deck comes through in this view across the panel of this C-97 on the ramp at Tucson. No fewer than 13 large windows are arranged on 2 tiers plus a further 2 eyebrow windows. Note the large pitch trim wheels and the thick emergency escape rope by the copilot's window.

Old

C-97s struggled on as the modern equivalent of tramp steamers until their temperamental powerplants often let them down. This aircraft was flying bread from La Paz, Baja, to the mainland on behalf of the Bimbo Bread Company. This Aeropacifico aircraft arrived at Tucson in February 1989 for an engine change and was still there nine years later!

On-Mark

Engineering of Van Nuys, California, modified the second Pan American Airways 377 for Aero Space Lines Corporation, which wanted a large volume aircraft capable of transporting large sections of space rockets to Florida for the Apollo program. The aircraft was lengthened by adding a 16-foot, 8-inch doughnut from another Stratocruiser before adding an enlarged upper fuselage structure. The result was the rather grotesque, but useful, Model 377-PG Pregnant Guppy. *Boeing*

The
bulbous planform of the Super Guppy is well illustrated in this overhead view of a NASA-owned example at the Pima County Air Museum in Arizona. Note the faired hinge and faintly visible join line around the crown of the fuselage where the nose swings open for loading and unloading.

Super
Guppies provided the vital links between the international partners in the Airbus consortium from 1971 until the last was retired in 1997. The new wing center section added to increase the Super Guppy's span by 15 feet is clearly visible in the photograph of Number 4 picking up its last load of Airbus wings (in this case a A319 for Swissair) at Manchester, England.

transporter was stretched by 16 feet, 8 inches. Then the upper fuselage was removed and a new 20-foot-high cargo area was built around a new lightweight roof structure. The outlandish looking aircraft was christened the Pregnant Guppy, and it was officially designated the 377-PG. The empty weight rose from the standard aircraft's 78,920 pounds to 91,000 pounds, but payload capability increased to 34,000 pounds.

The Pregnant Guppy was followed by new and more weird variants dubbed the Super Guppy and the Mini Guppy. The SG was 31 feet longer than the standard 377 and had a new center section that added an extra 15 feet to the wingspan. Unlike the first conversion, which hinged in the rear fuselage, the Super Guppy hinged through a joint at the nose and could carry cargo up to 25 feet, 6 inches in diameter for more than 30 feet of its length. The Mini Guppy conversions, on the other hand, hinged simply at the tail. The later modified SP aircraft were also re-engined with 4,912 shaft horsepower Allison 501-D22C turboprops.

The Super Guppy proved to be ideal for Airbus Industrie, which used the original pair of aircraft to shuttle subassemblies such as wings, tails, and fuselage sections, between its European partner companies. The workload grew to the extent that Airbus contracted Aeromaritime of France to convert two more aircraft for a fleet of four. The last of these was finally retired in 1997 when Airbus introduced a new jet-powered A300-600 transporter derivative called the Beluga. It was only then that Airbus could finally lay to rest the old joke that every Airbus jetliner began its life by riding in the belly of a Boeing! In the world of aerospace one of the most startling ironies will always be that a derivative of Boeing's last piston-engined product was vital to the birth of Airbus Industries' first jet, the A300, and to every subsequent member of the Airbus family until 1997.

The B-17G's four Wright R-1820-97 Cyclones each developed 1,200 horsepower at 25,000 feet. Weighing 65,500 pounds, the fully loaded B-17 could reach 20,000 feet in around 37 minutes.

3
Bomber Heritage

The threat of war, and war itself, was the force that propelled Boeing into its dominant position as king of the big jet builders during the second half of the twentieth century. In spite of the company's rapid progress in civil transports, the breakthrough into really large aircraft manufacturing, and the subsequent leap to big jets, came about through the demand for new bombers in the build-up to World War II.

Concerned by the rising tide of aggression around the world in the early 1930s, a group of visionaries within the U.S. Army Air Corps started to search for a new strategic bomber with the range and payload to defend far-off American territorial possessions such as Alaska and Hawaii. Japan's invasion of Manchuria and the growing tension in Europe caused by the rising power of the fascist leaders in Germany and Italy prompted the Air Corps to outline a bomber like none built before.

When aircraft makers, Boeing among them, were invited to bid on the secret project in April 1934, they were amazed at the colossal requirement. The Army Air Corps' seemingly modest requirement called for a "long-range airplane suitable for military purposes." Translated into facts and figures, the reality was extremely daunting. The Air Corps wanted an aircraft capable of flying 5,000 miles with a 2,000-pound bomb load and armed to the teeth for self-defense.

After meeting Air Corps chiefs at the Air Corps Materiel Division in Dayton, Ohio, in May 1934, a Boeing team led by Claire Egtvedt rushed back to Seattle to come up with a design proposal within the 30-day time limit.

The sheer size of the mission requirements called for a much larger aircraft than anything Boeing had designed before. Just making a wing large enough to carry sufficient fuel for a 5,000-mile round trip demanded thinking on a new scale. As always, the ambitions of the designers and planners outstripped the power available from the engines of the day, but Boeing believed that the planned 2,600-horsepower, 24-cylinder Allison V-3420 liquid-cooled engine would provide the necessary power. As a result, it outlined a four-engined design rather than being forced into more extreme measures such as the massive Dornier Do X flying boat that had been launched in 1929 with 12 engines (6 pushers and 6 pullers). Although wooden dummy Allison engines were mounted on the mockup, the real aircraft eventually flew with four 1,000-horsepower Pratt & Whitney R-1830-11 Twin Wasp twin-row radials.

To Boeing's joy, the Air Corps was impressed by the idea of its four-engined design, and by mid-1934 it was starting work under a $600,000 contract on the Experimental Bomber, Long Range or XBLR-1. Boeing assigned it Model 294, and by July 1936, more than a year before its first flight, the Air Corps reassigned

Twin 50-caliber machine guns sprout from a chin turret on this B-17G. The G countered a new head-on attack tactic developed by Luftwaffe pilots and made it into a true "Flying Fortress" by bringing the maximum number of machine guns to 13.

it with the more regular bomber designation of XB-15. As it came together, the big aircraft displayed many of the features that were to become an everyday aspect of successive Boeing generations. It was the first of the Boeing line to incorporate a "flight deck" for the pilot, copilot, navigator, and radio operator. As in all later big aircraft flight decks, the pilot and copilot had duplicate flight instruments with power and fuel instruments between the two positions. However, the flight deck also housed another crucial crew member—the flight engineer—who sat at a separate console and assisted the flight crew with the operation of the engines and other systems.

Other new features included bunks and a galley for the crew. Electrical power to help operate the aircraft's sophisticated systems came from two 110-volt AC generators driven by two auxiliary gasoline-powered engines. The aircraft's vast high-aspect-ratio wing was a record-breaking 149 feet in span, more than 3 feet greater than the 707, and wing area was an impressive 2,780 square feet. Construction was based largely on the by now traditional spar,

Passers-by on Marginal Way gape in wonder at the 149-foot wingspan of the XB-15, then the largest and heaviest aircraft ever built in the United States. The bomber, nicknamed "Grandpappy," never went into production, but the single prototype established several world records for weight carrying. It provided the basis for the wing of the Model 317 and the electrical system for the B-29, as well as invaluable "big plane" building experience for Boeing. *Boeing*

Y1B-17s of the 96th Bombardment Squadron make a classic picture as they pass over New York in 1937. By then the aircraft was powered by the famous Wright R-1820 Cyclone, and at the completion of this service test period, it was simply called the B-17. *Boeing*

stringer, and stressed skin methods and principles developed from the Monomail onwards. To save weight, however, the wing was metal skinned from the leading edge to the main spar and from roughly half chord aft was fabric covered. The deep wing section allowed a huge quantity of fuel to be carried and provided enough room for a small passageway along which the crew could crawl to inspect the engines in flight!

Almost exactly 42 months after the contract award, the lumbering monster made its first flight from Boeing Field on October 15, 1937, with test pilot Eddie Allen at the controls. The aircraft handled sedately and had few vices but proved to be underpowered. In view of its limi-

tations and because of its experimental nature, the two planned Y1B-20 service test models with more powerful R-2180 engines were never ordered. The sole XB-15 was used instead as a research and development aircraft and, when war broke out, was converted for cargo-carrying duties, with the designation XC-105. The aircraft did manage to break several world records, including carrying a 71,171-pound payload to 8,200 feet on July 30, 1939, but never achieved its intended operational potential.

Its biggest contribution, however, was to the overall development of the Boeing family tree. The sheer size of the XB-15 demanded the development of new manufacturing techniques and the production of huge tooling that

B-17s

gradually accumulated more fire power. This B-17E, pictured near Mount Rainier in 1942, is armed with guns in the tail as well as a Sperry-built ball turret beneath the belly. In action in the Pacific theater against the Japanese, the B-17Es surprised enemy fighter pilots who had faced earlier B-17 models without tail armament. *Boeing*

was to pay enormous dividends in future programs. It also pioneered Boeing's flight deck concept as well as paving the way for the long-range Model 314 and providing the circular fuselage cross-section, planform, engine arrangement, and rudder shape of one of the company's most famous products, the B-17 Flying Fortress.

FLYING FORTRESS

The same month as Egtvedt met with Air Corps officials over details of the XBLR-1 project, another competition was announced. In addition to the big bomber, the Air Corps wanted a smaller aircraft with a range of 1,020 miles, a 2,000-pound bomb load, a speed of 200 miles per hour and a crew of four to six. This time, however, there was no government money to offer. Entries for the multi-engined bomber competition were strictly at the expense and risk of each company, but the winner stood to get a production order for 220 aircraft.

Boeing's ingenuity was in its interpretation of "multi-engined." Boeing's chief competitors, Douglas and Martin, were designing twin-engined aircraft similar to most existing bomber designs at the time to meet the requirement (these were the B-18 and B-12, respectively). After

checking the small print, Boeing decided that multi-engined could just as easily mean three or even four engines. Boeing needed superior performance to win the competition. In terms of aerodynamics and structures, it had already reached maximum efficiency with design techniques honed to perfection on the B-9. This left engine power as the only remaining variable, and until now the number of engines simply reflected the power needed to meet the requirement. Boeing's innovation was to use more engines to go well beyond the requirement and hence win the competition.

The company needed to be sure it would win. The new aircraft, designated Model 299, cost a staggering $432,034, or nearly all the remaining cash reserve left to Boeing after the breakup of United Aircraft and Transport in 1934. The 299, therefore, became a huge gamble and one that would have to take place in secret as the design came together. Initial work began on June 18, 1934, with actual construction beginning on August 16.

When the aircraft was finally rolled out into the public eye at Boeing Field on July 1, 1935, it was quickly evident that the 299 was a cunning combination of the Model 247 (see chapter 2) and the yet-to-be-finished XB-15. Structurally and aerodynamically, it closely followed the clean lines of the airliner, yet the cross-section, planform, and defensive gun positions were borrowed directly from the bigger bomber. The dimensions of the aircraft, (103-foot, 9-inch span and 68-foot, 9-inch length) were also roughly midway between the 247 and XB-15. It is also said that the appearance of the 299, complete with five 30-caliber machine guns bristling from numerous blisters, also prompted one journalist to describe it as a "Flying Fortress," a name that would become an aviation legend.

The wide-span wing had an aspect ratio of 7.58 and was canted with an incidence angle of 3.5 degrees. The wing, which was swept back on the leading edge by 8.25 degrees, was made of two inner sections carrying the engine nacelles and two outer sections with detachable tips. The stressed-skin wings were also fitted with electrically operated split trailing-edge flaps. The flaps, ailerons, and other movable surfaces in the tail were covered in fabric. The fuselage, like the wing structure, was conventional, with a semi-monocoque design made up of bulkheads and circumferential stiffeners, tied together with longerons and longitudinal stiffeners. An unusual aspect of the design was the glazed nose section for the

Another famous example of the B-17's ruggedness is shown in this extraordinary photograph. A German Me-109 had collided in midair with the B-17F, which had been bombing supply lines in North Africa. With the entire empennage almost severed and one elevator missing altogether, the aircraft flew for another hour and a half back to its base, where it landed safely. The tail gunner, S/Sgt. Sam Sarpolus, described the journey like "riding on the end of a kite." *Boeing*

bombardier and nose gunner. This was gradually enlarged in later models.

The Model 299 (known to the Air Corps as the B-299 because it thought the Boeing designation of X-299 was too close to its own experimental aircraft designation system) made its first flight on July 28, 1935, with test pilot Les Towers at the controls. Powered by four Pratt & Whitney S1EG Hornet 750-horsepower engines, the 299 showed great promise. Initial tests revealed a maximum speed of 236 miles per hour, faster than most fighters of the day, and a cruising speed of 140 miles per hour at 70-percent power. This performance was underlined dramatically with a 9-hour delivery flight on August 20 from Seattle to Wright Field, Dayton, Ohio, where it was to take place in the bomber competition "fly-off" under the unofficial title of XB-17. The aircraft flew the 2,000 mile non-stop journey at an average air speed of 252 miles per hour and achieved ground speeds of 235 miles per hour.

Tests were going well when disaster struck on October 30. Les Tower and Major Pete Hill, chief of the Wright Field test pilots, were both killed when the aircraft crashed mysteriously on takeoff. A survivor, Lieutenant Donald Putt, helped in the inquiry that revealed the B-299 had taken off with the controls locked—another new feature that was introduced to prevent damage to the controls when the aircraft was sitting on the ground in gusty weather. Although the aircraft was technically exonerated, the B-299 had not completed its demonstration by the time of the crash, and the bad publicity was hard to ignore. To Boeing's dismay the contract went to the Douglas B-18. However, shortly afterwards, on January 17, 1936, the Air Corps gave the B-299 a second chance and ordered a small batch of "improved" versions designated the Model 299B, or Y1B-17.

The order for 13, plus the decision to go-ahead with the Model 307 Stratoliner, was enough to justify the construction of a new factory on the west side of Boeing Field. Although Boeing officials did not know it at the time, within a few years "Plant 2" would become the pumping heart behind the company's furious war effort with the B-17. In all, a total of 12,726 B-17s of all models were built, of which Boeing made 6,981. With mounting pressure on Boeing's factories, production of the bomber was also allocated to Vega Aircraft Corporation, a subsidiary of Lockheed based in Burbank, California, and to Douglas Aircraft in nearby Long Beach. Vega made 2,750 B-17s while Douglas, ironically the winner of the original competition, ended up making 2,995.

The ultimate production version of the aircraft was the B-17G. Powered by four Wright R-1820-97s producing 1,200 horsepower at 25,000 feet, the G could operate at gross weights up to 65,000 pounds compared to just over 38,000 pounds for the XB-17. Dimensionally the aircraft was largely unchanged, the major external differences being the large dorsal fin and modified tail that first appeared on the E model and different gun turrets in the nose and chin. Cruise speed was higher by 10 miles per hour at 150 miles per hour while the service ceiling had climbed by over 10,000 feet to the significantly more survivable altitude of 35,600 feet. Range had shrunk by more than 1,000 miles in exchange for much heavier defensive armaments (11 to 13 50-caliber machine guns) and a hugely increased bomb load of up to 9,600 pounds. Reflecting the changes, the B-17G's empty weight was more than 36,135 pounds, or almost 15,000 pounds more than the original XB-17.

This
remarkable series of pictures
shows a B-17F being accidentally
hit by bombs from another B-17
flying above it during a daylight
raid over Berlin. *Boeing*

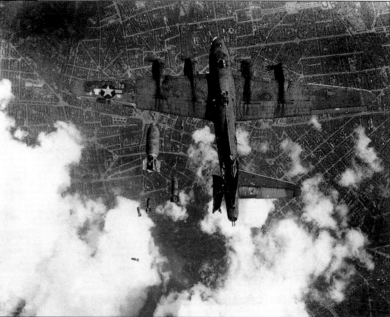

SUPERFORTRESS

The B-29 Superfortress truly became the aircraft that changed the world. On August 6, 1945, a B-29 named *Enola Gay* dropped the world's first atomic bomb on the Japanese city of Hiroshima, and three days later another B-29 called *Bockscar* dropped a second bomb on Nagasaki. The display of awesome power and the resulting devastation ended World War II and, in all likelihood, saved the carnage of a grueling land campaign in which possibly millions more lives would have been lost.

While the world at large has ample reason to record the B-29 in the history books, Boeing recognizes the aircraft for breakthroughs that are still relevant in the late 1990s. The B-29 was the first "big" aircraft over 100,000 pounds gross weight to go into mass production using new assembly techniques that remain essentially unchanged to this day. The aircraft and much of the technology it pioneered set the "big plane" foundation on which Boeing would build its air transport lineage.

Unlike the other military aircraft produced by Boeing, the B-29 did not originate with a specific requirement. Its tangled roots can be traced to March 1938 when Boeing began studies of a pressurized version of the B-17 with the model number 334. Although requested by the Air Corps, funding was short, so Boeing kept it going with company money. By July 1939, the study was further refined as the 334A, and within five months Boeing was so convinced it was on the right track that it began construction of a company-funded mockup.

At this point outside events overtook the 334A when in January 1940 the Air Corps issued a requirement for a "Superbomber." War Department Data Request R-40B called for a four-engined bomber that could fly a round-trip mission of 5,333 miles and deliver a 2,000-pound bomb load. The new bomber would need to operate at altitudes over 30,000 feet and fly at the incredible speed of between 300 and 400 miles per hour. In response, Boeing dusted off some of the elements developed for the 334A, such as the pressurization and self-defense weapon systems, and rolled it into a much larger airframe dubbed the Model 345. The study was submitted to the Air Corps on May 11, 1940, and attracted enough interest from the military to win some development money for further wind-tunnel tests.

Finally, on August 24, Boeing was awarded a $3.61 million contract to build two prototypes and a third for

static test. The XB-29, or Superfortress, as Boeing called it, was officially launched with this deal and within two weeks the contract was amended to include a third flying prototype. More changes were to come. In May 1941 the B-29, although not even built by then, made its mark on U.S. aviation history when the Army ordered the staggering total of 250 "paper" airplanes straight off the drawing board. Pushed largely by General Henry "Hap" Arnold, the contract covered the building of the new bomber at Boeing's Wichita site in Kansas and was upped to 500 in January 1942, the month after Japan's attack on the U.S. Navy at Pearl Harbor in Hawaii. The move to build the aircraft away from Seattle partially reflected a concern that the U.S. West Coast was vulnerable to Japanese attack and was augmented by a new order in February 1942 that specified the setting up of new lines around the country. These included one at Bell in Marietta, Georgia; North American at Kansas City; and the Fisher Body Division of General Motors at Cleveland, Ohio. To ensure added protection, the roofs over Boeing's vast assembly buildings in the Seattle area were extensively camouflaged to look from the air like suburbs.

The U.S. government's $3 billion gamble on Boeing's new Superfortress was put to the test for the first time on September 21, 1942, when the prototype XB-29 made its maiden flight under tight security from Boeing Field with Eddie Allen as the engineering test pilot. To the few outsiders who glimpsed the huge-looking aircraft, there seemed to be no obvious similarities with the B-17. They were right. Other than the empennage, which was virtu-

The high aspect ratio (11.5:1) of the slender Boeing-designed 117 wing section was key to the excellent performance of the B-29. Here the impressive 141-foot, 3-inch span is displayed as the Confederate Air Force's "Fifi" turns over the Texas scrub.

ally a simple scale-up of the B-17, there was virtually nothing in common between the two.

As with the XB-15, Boeing quickly recognized that something far more radical was required to meet the demanding specification set out in R-40B. The main requirement was for a huge wing that would allow the big bomber to cruise far, high, and fast with a big payload. The result was a surprisingly slender-looking wing with a massive span of 141 feet, 3 inches and an aspect ratio (span to chord ratio) of 11.5. The Boeing wing section, numbered 117, represented a major leap over anything in the past, including the B-17's older technology airfoil, which had, for example, utilized classic NACA-designed wing sections ranging from 0018 at the root to 0010 at the tip.

The problem with long, thin wings is the relatively high wing loading incurred. Simply translated this means the thinner the wing, for a given span, the smaller the wing surface area available to carry the load. With the high take-off and operating weights expected of the bomber this caused the Army Air Corps engineers to question the veracity of the wing design that had been led by George Schairer. The B-29 wing was essentially being asked to support almost twice the weight per square foot of wing as the B-17. Boeing, however, persisted and convinced the skeptics that increasing the chord and wing area would

produce a much heavier and higher drag structure. This, in turn, would be unable to perform the mission without much higher powered engines, and the planned power-plant for the bomber, the untried 2,200-horsepower Wright R-3350, was already the largest then available.

Another design feature that helped Boeing win the day was the incorporation of huge Fowler-type flaps on the trailing edge of the wing. These were the largest flaps yet developed and, when extended by the electrically driven actuation system, increased wing area by a dramatic 19 percent. To increase the effective area, the flaps were also extended into contoured sections that covered the aft part of the inboard engine cowlings, thereby ensuring the maximum use of trailing-edge flap. The leading edge was swept back by 7 degrees, slightly less than the B-17, but shared the same 4.5-degree dihedral.

To enable the vast wings to be built on the existing production lines, they were assembled from one large center section extending outboard of the engines with the two outer sections and detachable wing tips added later. To keep drag to a minimum, the all-metal web-type structure was covered with a flush riveted butt-joined metal skin.

Another subtle but vital innovation was in the construction of the fuselage. The war effort, plus the sheer size of the B-29, demanded newer, faster, and more efficient

Staggered
waist gun positions were introduced
on later models, like the B-17G, after
gunners found they got in each
other's way during combat.

"Texas Raider"
makes an impressive sight as it climbs
out against the billowing smoke from
a mock Japanese bombing raid. The
supercharger that made all the
difference to the performance of the
B-17 is just visible at the aft end of the
number four engine nacelle nearest
the camera.

construction methods. Ironically some of the advanced manufacturing concepts used on the B-29 were derived from the design of a German bomber, the Heinkel He-111. One of the bombers had been captured intact by the British and, after government and industry experts had looked it over, it had been shipped to the United States for similar evaluation. One of the key lessons was the construction of the fuselage, which was riveted at the skin joints allowing major sub-assemblies to be put together quickly even with unskilled workers. The "production joint" method was therefore adopted, eliminating the need for splicing the longitudinal stringers that form the fore and aft strengthening structure of all conventionally built aircraft. The innovation was a major breakthrough that was to be used to great effect on all of Boeing's succeeding big aircraft. In another ironic twist Boeing's evaluation of the He 111 structure also revealed it to be a virtual carbon copy of its own Model 247, particularly the tail area.

By means of the new techniques, the B-29 fuselage was made up of five major sub-assemblies. Each was built from a series of circumferential bulkheads and frames, with extruded longerons and stringers and a flush-riveted and butt-jointed stressed-metal skin. Small clips with pre-punched, full-size rivet holes tied the "former" to the stringers, which were also pre-formed with matching holes. The fuselage was also pressurized in three areas: the forward section, the area aft of the bomb bay, and a small section in the tip of the tail. This was a lonely spot for the tail gunner as it was completely isolated from the rest of the aircraft during the pressurized segment of the mission. The two forward pressurized sections were, however, connected with a pressurized crawl tunnel, which ran along the aircraft's spine over the two bomb bays.

Another unusual feature was the introduction, for the first time on any aircraft, of remote-controlled gun turrets. The imperative to reduce drag wherever possible, the high operating altitudes of the B-29, and the complexities of pressurization quickly ruled out the use of standard turrets like those of the B-17. Instead, the aircraft was fitted with four General Electric remotely controlled and electrically operated turrets, each armed with two 50-caliber machine guns, two above and two below the fuselage. The Bell-made aft turret gave the B-29 a real sting in its tail with one 20-mm cannon and two 50-caliber guns. The guns were aimed and controlled from five sighting stations, one in the nose, one in the tail, and three in the middle pressurized compartment. Some stations had secondary control

over other turrets, but only one sight was in control of a given turret at one time.

As briefly mentioned, the size of the B-29 required the biggest engines available. These were the untried 2,200-horsepower Wright R-3350-23 18-cylinder air-cooled radials. The engines drove huge 16-foot, 7-inch-diameter Hamilton Standard Hydromatic four-blade full-feathering propellers through gearing that turned the propeller shaft 35 times for every 100 revolutions of the crankshaft. To get every possible ounce of power from the engines at high altitude, each was also fitted with two General Electric exhaust-driven turbo-superchargers, one mounted on either side of the nacelle. Problems with the complicated engines plagued the flight tests and early service life of the B-29 and led to the loss of the second XB-29 prototype on February 18, 1943. The aircraft, piloted by Eddie Allen, was attempting to return to Boeing Field with an out-of-control engine fire when it crashed on a meat packing factory in South Seattle, killing all 11 crew and 24 on the ground.

Despite the persistent engine problems, initial B-29 production got under way at Wichita, Kansas, where 14 initial service test YB-29s were manufactured. Production was also started at Bell's facility in Marietta, but aircraft due to be made at the Fisher Body production site in Cleveland were switched to Martin's factory in Omaha, Nebraska. Production of PBB-1 Sea Rangers for the U.S. Navy was switched to Kansas City allowing Boeing's Renton factory to become a center for B-29A production.

With Allied forces poised to launch the Normandy invasion in Europe, the B-29 began its service career on the other side of the world on June 5, 1944, with an attack on rail yards in Bangkok, Thailand, launched from bases in India. Ten days later bombers from four secret bases in China dropped their bombs on steel mills in Yawata, Japan. Attacks on the Japanese mainland were steadily stepped up as Allied forces recaptured territory in the Pacific and were able to launch missions from bases closer to Japan in the Marianas and on Guam.

After the defeat of Japan some 5,092 B-29s still on order were canceled, though a few in advanced stages of production were completed. In all, total B-29 production amounted to 3,627 with the last aircraft delivered on June 10, 1946. The bomber was to see further active service in the Korean war, and 87 were loaned to the RAF as "Washingtons" in 1950. Many saw service in special roles such as tanker aircraft, and photo and weather reconnaissance, the last WB-29 being retired in 1960.

A lone B-17 flies in salute over London's Big Ben clock tower to mark the 50th anniversary of Victory in Europe (VE) day. The Royal Air Force was the first to use the Fortress in combat when a force of B-17Cs was sent on a daylight raid on Brest, France, on July 24, 1941. The aircraft's biggest association with England, however, was the vast number that operated for the United States Eighth Air Force. The "Mighty Eighth" lost a staggering 4,754 B-17s and 2,112 B-24 Liberators during the war, which claimed the lives of 44,472 U.S. aircrew. RAF bomber losses were 10,724 aircraft and 55,573 aircrew.

OPPOSITE

B-29As roll off the line at Boeing's Renton factory. The factory was originally built by the U.S. Navy to make the PBB-1 Sea Ranger but changed over to the B-29 when the patrol aircraft was scrapped. A total of 3,627 B-29s were built. *Boeing*

In the classic setting of an air base "somewhere in England," this B-17 is painted up to represent *Memphis Belle*. One of the most famous aircraft of World War II, *Memphis Belle* was the first Eighth Air Force B-17 to complete 25 combat missions over Europe. The 25th mission was filmed in 1943 by William Wyler and is acknowledged as a masterpiece of documentary making to this day.

B-50 LAST OF THE LINE

The B-29 family had one more direct contribution to make to the Boeing family tree before it was finished—the B-50. Although externally nothing more than a B-29 with a bigger tail and engines, the B-50 was so full of improvements that it represented a 75-percent all-new aircraft. The program began as a re-engining exercise when one of the 14 YB-29 test fleet was handed over to General Motors for installation of liquid-cooled Allison V-3420-11 engines. The experiment with the XB-39, as it was called, came to nothing but was followed by tests of another engine, the four-row 28-cylinder Pratt & Whitney R-4360. A standard B-29A was converted into the XB-44 test bed for the trials, which proved so successful when they began in May 1945 that two months later the Air Force ordered 200. Within weeks the victory over Japan reduced the order for B-29Ds, as they had become, to just 60.

Not to be outdone, Boeing cleverly changed the designation to B-50 in December 1945. The new name gave the impression of a more modern design and distracted interest away from the B-29, which had been canceled. The vast amount of new features in the B-50 gave the company some justification for its cunning ploy, which eventually resulted in a total of 371 valuable orders and continuous production to 1953. The heart of the B-50 was its powerful 3,500-horsepower Pratt & Whitney R-4360-35 Wasp Major engines that gave a power increase of 59 percent over the B-29. More power enabled the B-50A's gross weight to top out at almost 169,000 pounds compared to the earlier aircraft's 105,000 pounds (before post-World War II modifications). Heavier weight required the flaps to be enlarged and the tail to be increased in height almost 5 feet to 32 feet, 8 inches. The larger fin exceeded the truss height of many U.S. military hangars, so it was hinged at the base to allow it to be folded down. This feature reappeared on the B-52 and was even discussed as an option for the 747 design.

Other improvements were made beneath the skin, which itself was upgraded with a move to a newer type of aluminum called 75 ST. Compared to the B-29's conventional 24 ST skin, the B-50's was 16-percent stronger, 26 percent more efficient, and 650 pounds lighter. The undercarriage, which was slow to retract on the B-29, could now be brought up into the bay in 11 seconds, thanks to a new ball-screw mechanism. The older, maintenance-intensive rubber de-icer boots were also replaced with a hot-air de-icing system, which channeled exhaust from combustion heaters in the engine nacelles and fin to the leading edges of the empennage and wings. Maneuvering was also improved with the addition of nosewheel steering and hydraulic rudder boost.

Further improvements were planned for yet another variant, dubbed the B-54, which was canceled when it

became obvious that piston-power was obsolete and jets were the way of the future. The B-50, which soldiered on in several roles as trainers, flying tankers, and reconnaissance aircraft, was finally retired from military service in 1964, marking the end of Boeing's enduring piston-bomber link with the Air Force.

STRATOJET—THE JET REVOLUTION

The B-47 played a pivotal role in Boeing's development. Its revolutionary lines propelled both the company and the U.S. Air Force bomber fleet into the jet age and established the blueprint from which all Boeing's success in jetliners was derived.

Key to the entire project was the availability of a new form of high-speed propulsion called the gas turbine, or jet engine. Developed almost in parallel in great secrecy in Germany and England, jet technology arrived in the United States in 1941 when the British government gave America design details of the Whittle W.1 turbojet. Due to its expertise with high-temperature-resistant metals developed for the superchargers used in the B-17 and B-29, General Electric was given responsibility for producing the first U.S.-made jets. The resulting I-16 turbojet engines were fitted into a simple airframe built for the purpose by Bell, called the XP-59A Airacomet, which flew for the first time on October 1, 1942.

Flight testing took place, again in top secret, at a remote base at Muroc dry lakebed (later Edwards AFB) in California. It was here that Boeing and other contractors were invited in 1943 to discuss the use of the revolutionary powerplants on medium bomber and reconnaissance aircraft. Boeing's Ed Wells and George Schairer were among the first to see "what they could make using these jet engines, which were sure great gas hogs," recalled Schairer. Boeing drew up study plans of a four-engined Model 424, which resembled a smaller version of the B-29. "It had a straight wing, very thin. I think it was 10-percent thick, had big nacelles, each with two engines in it, and the landing gear retracted into them. A rather pure vanilla airplane," said Schairer.

Competing designs from Convair (XB-46), Glenn Martin (XB-48), and North American (XB-45) were essentially similar, and other than the Martin design (which had six engines) all the manufacturers quickly discovered that: "They couldn't carry the bomb. They were too small." In an effort to compensate for the power limitations of the small jets (around 4,000 pounds thrust maximum) and therefore the restricted size of the airframe, Boeing recognized the need for a drastically improved lift/drag ratio over the B-17/B-29. "We wanted to go fast," said Schairer, "and we had a tool which none of our competitors had . . . we had this wind tunnel." The facility was the brain child of Eddie Allen but had been led by Bill Cook. Built at the then astounding cost of $750,000, the 18,000-horsepower engine drove a 24-foot-diameter fan to create speeds up to 0.975 Mach in the 8x12-foot test section of the tunnel. The transonic test facility was opened in 1944.

Using wind-tunnel data, Boeing redesigned the jet bomber with the engines buried in the body to improve the efficiency of the wing. The Air Force was sufficiently impressed to award a Phase I study contract for Boeing's Model 432 aimed at the new XB-47 bomber. But even Boeing was not happy with the 432. The undercarriage arrangement was awkward, and there were concerns that the engine location was too dangerous. Ken Holtby, who was assigned as the Air Force project and contracting officer for the XB-47, recalled that at Wright Field, in Dayton, Ohio, "we had been running a test in the big wind tunnel back there of a P-80 with holes in the jet engine burners that simulated 50-caliber bullet holes. We managed to get about an 18-inch blowtorch out of that holed aluminum in about 2

seconds." The demonstration was shown to Ed Wells and Bob Jewett of Boeing. "Ed started drawing pictures on the way home of pod-mounted engines."

In April 1945 a United States Army exploitation team in war-torn Germany made a breakthrough that changed everything for Boeing. A team led by physicist Theodore von Karman discovered, buried in the records of the Reichmarshal Hermann Goering Aeronautical Research Institute, German research documents that explained the theoretical background to the successful use of swept wings. These had been used in conjunction with both jet and rocket power to produce two of the most aerodynamically advanced aircraft of the war, the Messerschmitt Me 262 Schwalbe and the Me 163 Komet. George Schairer, one of three Boeing engineers on the team, instantly realized that this was the answer to Boeing's quest for more speed on the embryonic XB-47. He sent a message back to Seattle instructing the design team to stop work on the straight-wing concept and embrace the idea of a swept design.

By sweeping the angle of the wing sharply forward or aft, the data showed that the formation of shock waves was delayed. This enabled the aircraft, for the same amount of power, to fly faster.

The first swept-wing designs began tests in the Boeing wind tunnel that August, and shortly after, convinced it had the right ingredients, the company asked for a one-year delay in the competition to incorporate the new feature. The Air Force program officials were skeptical. "They believed that putting sweep on a bomber airplane was kind of a wild idea, and they considered Schairer to be an eccentric genius that needed rather close supervision," remembered Holtby. The move nearly led to the cancellation of the entire program, but a further meeting with Wells and Jewett convinced them that an extension would bring huge benefits. The Air Force and Boeing reluctantly agreed to refine a revised design, still incorporating the buried engines, called the Model 448. The big difference this time was the 35-degree wing-sweep angle, measured at the quarter chord point.

After the Air Force expressed concerns over the vulnerability of the body-mounted powerplants, the final design was revised to incorporate both swept wings and six pod-mounted engines. Another feature was the unusual bicycle or tandem landing gear arrangement. This had been evaluated earlier in 1945 by Martin on a modified XB-26H Marauder nicknamed the Mid-River Stump

This
B-29 was rescued from China Lake Naval Weapons Test Range in California, where it had been dumped as a target. Today the "Dreamboat," as the B-29s were nicknamed, is resplendently preserved at the Seattle Museum of Flight, where it was lovingly restored by volunteers, many of whom worked on the original production line.

B-29s

could take plenty of hits. One was hit by flak over Osaka, Japan. With half the nose shot away it went into a spiral dive before the surviving, but badly injured, copilot pulled it out at 10,000 feet. Without instruments, the crippled B-29 headed roughly in the direction of Iwo Jima. Nearly 4 hours later a P-61 Black Widow luckily intercepted the lost bomber and guided it to the island, which it would have missed by 100 miles. The surviving crew bailed out, and the P-61 crew was ordered to shoot the B-29 down, which it did, after using 450 rounds of ammunition! "We had never heard of an aircraft absorbing such punishment," said the radar observer, Lt. Arvid Shulenberger.

Jumper. The vital reason for this was that more space was created in the fuselage for a continuous bomb bay capable of carrying an atomic weapon. Before the emergence of the final winning design, Model 450, Boeing also added an 8-foot wing-tip extension to each tip, increasing the span to 116 feet and the aspect ratio slightly to 9.43.

The Air Force approved the design in October 1945, and in April 1946 Holtby signed a contract with Boeing worth $9.7 million for two experimental XB-47s, including spares and mockups. The first aircraft rolled out on September 12, 1947, and caused a sensation with its sleek lines and futuristic look. Big jets with swept wings had never been seen before in either military or civil guise, and the B-47 was the first of all of them. The gleaming silver machine supported six 3,750-pound-thrust General Electric J-35 turbojets hung in pods under the wing. Two pairs were strut-mounted inboard, and the single engines were attached directly to the lower wing surface well outboard. The tandem gear and outrigger wheels projecting from below the inboard engine nacelles added further to the outlandish appearance.

Boeing's bold move into largely uncharted design territory was to be rewarded with good luck in most cases and cunningly solved problems in others. Detractors of swept wings claimed the B-47 would be unable to meet the Air Force's exacting range requirement because of the decreased span, increased weight, and reduced fuel capacity. In the event, the extremely high wing loading (105 pounds per square foot) was compensated by the wing's design tendency to "wash out" loads at the tip and the bending moment relief of the underslung engines. The slender wing did not need immense strengthening and was efficient, allowing the

bomber to carry a 22,000-pound warload over more than 2,000 nautical miles.

Some unforeseen aspects of the wing sweep were realized well after the design was frozen, but fortunately the configuration was as perfect as it would have been had Boeing engineers been aware of the issue. One concerned the stiffness of the aircraft structure and particularly the effect of the wing-tip "unloading," causing the center of lift to quickly move forward, resulting in potentially violent instability. Due to the sweep, the wing tips were about halfway back to the tail, so when they deflected, they had the same effect as elevators. Luckily the bending motion of the body and the resulting angle of the stabilizer worked together to compensate almost seamlessly.

Other motions or aeroelastic characteristics of the flexible aircraft proved less forgiving. Flight tests began on December 17, 1947, and quickly revealed the phenomenon of aileron reversal. This was a well-known condition in straight-winged aircraft where, under certain circumstances, the deflection of the aileron actually twisted the wing itself. This led to the wing tip acting like a huge aileron, rolling the aircraft in the opposite direction. But the swept wing was something new, and Boeing was again in uncharted aeronautical waters.

"The first analyses that were done on the B-47 on this problem simply didn't account for one factor that happens on a swept wing, and that is that when you put a bending load on the wing, you put the aileron down," said Holtby. "That causes the wing to bend up, which reduces the angle of attack, putting a load in the other direction and counteracting the aileron load." The aerodynamicists computed the new roll rates and reversal speeds and tried various fixes. Out of their experiments came spoilers—a feature of every subsequent Boeing jet design. "The spoiler was located in the middle of the wing. That does two things for you. First, it does not impose a big torsional (twisting) load on the wing. Second, by putting it further inboard, it also imposes a lower bending load on the wing so that you sort of kill two birds with one stone. We were learning a great deal," remembered Holtby. "We had this great big floppy, flexible airplane that we didn't understand very well, but we learned an awful lot."

The B-47 also proved susceptible to "Dutch roll," a condition in which the aircraft rocks slowly in yaw, or from side to side. Boeing developed a yaw "damper" that automatically compensated for the motion by

OPPOSITE
Another innovation of the B-29 design was this crawl tube, seen here running above the bomb bay, which connected the pressurized crew compartment in the tail to the cockpit area visible through the open hatch.

The adoption of a fully glazed nose was an evolutionary leap beyond the B-17 and resembled the Heinkel He-111, one of which had been captured by the British and shipped to the United States for examination early in the war. The pilot's controls and instruments are separated from those of the copilots to allow access to the nose for the bomb aimer. The Norden bombsight is visible to the right.

adjusting the rudder. William "Bill" Cook, XB-47 aerodynamics unit chief, described the first device as a "makeshift contraption." Ed Pfaffman, a controls engineer on the program, "went down to the junk yard and got an amplifier from the turbo waste-gate control on a B-29. He got a gyro with electric pick-off from the Honeywell Company, and he got a transformer to match the two and a servo motor," said Cook. The

device, nicknamed "Little Herbert," became a standard feature on every Boeing jetliner built since.

Another problem the test team discovered was flow separation of the shock wave over the outboard sections of the wing when the crew pulled 1 g during high-speed turns or when changing course at Mach 0.75. In all early-design, fast subsonic jets, the airflow over the wing surface would accelerate quickly to the speed of sound, forming a shock wave. The problem with the B-47 wing was that this shock wave would suddenly detach, causing a dramatic loss of lift. As the loss was closer to the wing tips, the lift loss was behind the center of gravity, causing the jet to suddenly pitch up. The pilot was then forced to correct by getting the nose down and reducing the speed. As this was clearly unacceptable, Boeing went looking for a solution.

The answer lay in small, stublike vanes called vortex generators. These 1-inch-long projections rose up from the wing surface by up to an inch. Their job was to punch through the "boundary layer" of rough air that was slowed by friction with the wing skin and to swirl the flow of "laminar" air passing just above it. The swirl, or vortex, trapped energy back into the lower layer and prevented it from suddenly detaching from the wing altogether. The exact positioning of the "Vgs" as they were called, was

something of a black art as they had never been fitted on a Boeing-built aircraft before. With wind-tunnel data and a measure of good luck, Boeing got the locations of the Vgs almost right the first time. They were set in two rows on a section over the outboard engine nacelle, with the first row set at around 20-percent chord and the second at around 35 percent. The front Vgs were half an inch high, and the aft devices were an inch high.

Boeing aerodynamacist Bob Brown was chiefly responsible for the Vg locations. These were tested on wind-tunnel models before being attached to the real thing. At first the test team was concerned because the models showed no flow improvement. "Well, we did a flight test, and magically, the first installation we tried showed a major, major improvement," said Brown. The flying qualities improved so much that the B-47 could easily be handled by regular USAF pilots and not just highly qualified test pilots.

Test pilots "Tex" Johnston and Dick Taylor were the first to fly the aircraft with the Vgs. Brown recalled that Tex was not convinced the devices would do anything to solve the high-speed instability problem. The test began with a dive from 40,000 feet. "Then we knew he was pushing it over in a dive, and all we could hear was the breathing through his voice mask. It was moderate to heavy breathing. He got down to 35,000 feet and said, 'I'm going to go up and try that again,' and I said, 'Hmm . . . maybe something happened.' And so he went up and tried it again, and next time he came down whatever had happened, it happened again. He said, 'Brown, I don't know what you did,

but you did something.' So that was the first announcement that we had gone a major way to fixing the high-speed instability and pitch-up of the airplane."

During the early tests to find exactly the right location of the Vgs, the crew fitted a 35-mm camera to the tail fin to record pictures of cotton tufts, which were stuck to the wing to help visualize flow patterns. Dick Taylor recalled that a Wichita movie theater had to be rented to watch the films. "We went down to the movie house, but it was a classified program, and the fellow up in the projection room couldn't watch the screen, so he had to operate the machine and somebody stand there and tell him which way to turn it to get it in focus."

Another new problem with the sleek jet was its long landing distance. The early jet engines had extremely slow response times, for example, the J-47 engines took 30 seconds to spool up from full idle thrust to full power, and so approaches were flown at high-thrust setting. Approach speed at 100,000 pounds was 140 miles per hour, and touchdown speed was around 136. With reverse thrust and anti-skid brakes still in the future, braking was not allowed above 95 miles per hour, and stopping distance from a 50-foot obstacle was 8,365 feet. The best ground roll ever recorded by the test team was 5,940 feet on a dry runway, so something had to be done.

Boeing again turned captured German technology from World War II to its advantage, this time using a high-strength ribbon parachute originally developed to help brake the Arado Ar 234 "Blitz" jet bomber. A 32-foot-diameter deceleration parachute was eventually

Compared to its prop-driven contemporaries, the swept wing, clean lines, and clustered jets of the XB-47 created a sensation when it was first unveiled in September 1947. The thin wing is clearly illustrated in this nose-on view of the aircraft high over Moses Lake, Washington, in 1948. "The whole wing would quiver when you put the gear up" recalled test pilot Guy Townsend. *Boeing*

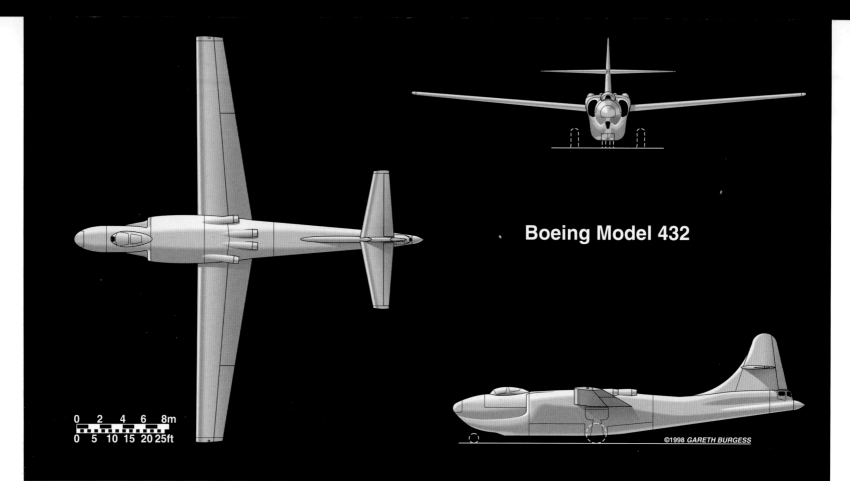

Boeing Model 432

©1998 *GARETH BURGESS*

The

Boeing Model 432 was an early, straight-winged concept for the new XB-47 bomber. While the design had some merits, it was abandoned because the engine placement was not considered safe and its landing gear arrangement was awkward. *Gareth Burgess*

installed under the B-47 tail as a result, while a secondary drogue chute was also fitted to act as an inflight air brake. The drogue chute could be jettisoned if the aircraft had to go around and sufficient power was available from the engines. Crews eventually developed a technique for deploying the main chute while still a few feet above the runway.

To augment takeoff performance, the B-47 was also fitted with 18 solid propellant JATO (jet-assisted takeoff) rockets inside the fuselage aft of the wing. The rockets added an extra 18,000 pounds of thrust for takeoff and, instead of being jettisoned after use as they had been on the World War II bombers and flying boats for which they had been originally developed, they were retained in the fuselage. With the use of the more powerful 7,200-pound-thrust J-47-GE-25 engines later in the B-47E model, the internal JATO system was replaced with a jettisonable rack containing 33 1,000-pound-thrust rockets.

With Cold War tensions on the rise, the B-47 quickly assumed top priority status. As a result, the Boeing-Douglas-Lockheed production pool set up during World War II was re-established for the jet bomber. By the time production ceased in 1956 some 2,032

B-47s had been built. Of these, 1,373 were made by Boeing, 274 by Douglas, and 385 by Lockheed. Although tactically beneficial to Douglas and Lockheed as useful contract work, the strategic winner was, of course, Boeing. The B-47 pioneered so many new features from swept wings and podded jets to flight control and stability know-how that its true importance to Boeing and its eventual dominance of the jetliner business cannot be overstated.

B-52 STRATOFORTRESS

Of all the Boeing jets, the B-52 has perhaps one of the strangest beginnings. Conceived by a group of engineers over an intensive weekend in a Dayton hotel room, the bomber would eventually become America's longest serving front-line combat aircraft.

In June 1946 Boeing was awarded a study contract for a long-range heavy bomber designated the XB-52. A new technology turboprop engine was considered the best bet for the new bomber because jet engines were too thirsty to meet the projected range requirement. Boeing's Model 462 was therefore a relatively conventional straight-wing design with six 5,500-horsepower Wright T-35 turboprops later revised to four improved versions offering

Boeing Model 448

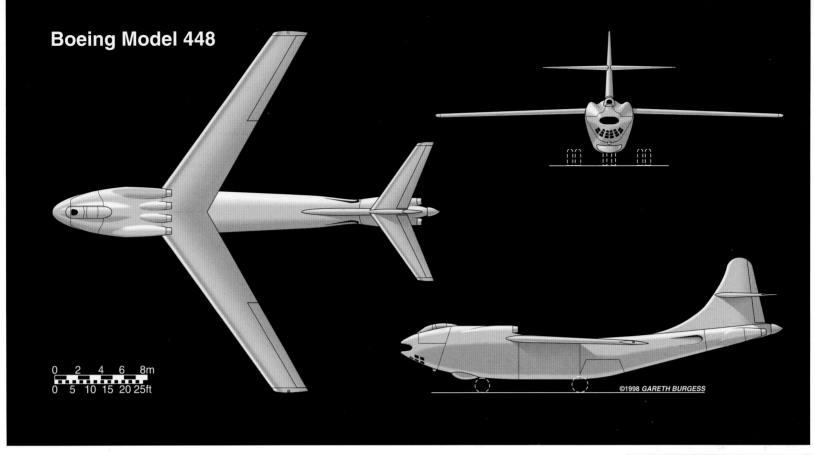

0 2 4 6 8m
0 5 10 15 20 25ft

©1998 *GARETH BURGESS*

8,900 horsepower and more range. But Boeing's growing love affair with jets was proving hard to resist, and parallel to the turboprop studies, it privately funded a pure-jet study of its own.

The decision was wise, as events proved in October 1948 at a review meeting with the USAF at Wright Field. Boeing was told the turboprop was already outmoded and that the XB-52 would be canceled unless the company could come up with something better, possibly using Pratt & Whitney's new J57 jet engine. George Schairer, who was part of the team, recalled that they retired to their Dayton hotel room and asked, "What can we do?' So that weekend we drew an airplane. We took the airplane that Bob Withington [leader of the parallel jet study] had been wind-tunnel testing and increased all the dimensions about 50 percent. We put on eight engines instead of the four engines; we made drawings of it; we made weight estimates of the airplane. I went down and bought a bunch of balsa wood and made a model of the airplane; we made drawings of it. Come Monday morning we went out to Wright Field to the Air Force and said, 'Okay . . . here's our proposal. Here's an airplane. We propose to convert our B-52 contract to building an eight-engined jet airplane, and here's all the data on it, all done over a weekend.'"

The team's feverish industry was rewarded with the authorization of new design studies. "Everybody says it was just a weekend wonder," said Schairer, "but it wasn't. It was the result of all the tremendous work that had gone forward in the flight testing of the B-47 and all the work that Bob Withington and others had been doing on how would you do better than that." After several close shaves, in which the contract was actually canceled more than once, Boeing was awarded a contract for two prototypes. The first of these rolled out of the final assembly at Plant 2 on a cold, wet night in November 1951. Despite the timing of the roll out (at night around Thanksgiving) and the huge white covers draped across the bomber to hide its shape and keep it dry, there was no hiding the shared heritage with the B-47.

Overall configuration was very similar with pod-mounted engines beneath a large wing with a sweep-back angle of 35 degrees. The tandem-gear arrangement with outriggers was also retained, though the much heavier bomber required four main gears rather than the B-47's two. These individually retracted twin-wheel main units retracted fore and aft of the bomb bay and could be set at a selected degree of castor in flight

T̲his rather ugly bomber concept represents a critical turning point in the history of Boeing design. Utilizing technology exploited from Germany during World War II, Boeing adapted swept-wing technology to its XB-47 concept and developed the Model 448. The 35-degree wing sweep, measured at the quarter chord point, would enable the bomber to fly faster than a straight wing aircraft with the same amount of power.
Gareth Burgess

Early jet engines, like the GE J-47s used on the B-47, were slow to accelerate so were supplemented with 18 solid propellant JATO (jet assisted takeoff) rockets. These were built into the fuselage and added an enormous 18,000 pounds of thrust for a few vital seconds. Later models, from the B-47E onwards, could be fitted with a jettisonable rack containing 33 1,000-pound-thrust rockets. Here a B-47 literally rockets into the air at Kirtland AFB, New Mexico, in 1950. *Boeing*

The underslung engines and 35-degree swept-back, laminar-flow Boeing 145 aerofoil of the B-47 provided the blueprint for virtually all subsequent Boeing jet-powered designs. Here a Strategic Air Command B-47E poses for the camera. Note the 1,500-gallon auxiliary fuel tanks under each wing. *Boeing*

or on the ground for crosswind landings. The big bomber would need big runways, and Boeing figured there were simply too few military bases with sufficiently large multiple runways to cope with different wind directions, so the movable gear would allow the B-52 to "crab" on the approach, with the wheels lined up with the strip.

The wing itself, however was significantly improved over the B-47. "The wing was very much refined and had better aerodynamic characteristics and was very much lighter than anything we'd been able to do on the B-47," said Schairer. "We found out, for instance, that we could make the center part of the wing very much thicker than we thought We thought this part of the wing would be a big problem to us, so we had made it very thin wing saved a lot of weight and gave us a place to put some fuel." As a result, the thickness taper was not constant and ranged from a Boeing 233 aerofoil at the root and a Boeing 236 at the tip. Looking aft, the upper and lower wing surfaces actually appeared to be convex rather than following a conventional taper to the tip.

Another improvement was in the flight controls, which had proved so troublesome with the B-52's predecessor. "We learned how to put much better lateral controls on for making the wings roll and how to get the control forces down to levels the pilots would like. This was a great refinement over the B-47," said Schairer. The flight controls were originally based around flaperons (flaps and ailerons combined), but these soon proved inadequate, and lateral control was achieved by the use of serrated spoilers, which doubled as speed brakes, on the upper wing surfaces. To assist with pitch control and trim, the entire horizontal tail could be moved. This feature was a first for a big jet and was to become common on all the subsequent jetliners.

The first aircraft that rolled out on November 29, 1951, the five-seat XB-52, did not fly until almost a year later. The first flight was made, instead, by the second aircraft, designated the YB-52. This rolled out on March 15, 1952, and flew one month later. The first production model, a B-52A, flew on August 5, 1954, and differed from the prototypes in having a modified nose section containing a flight deck instead of tandem

A long-retired Cold War warrior bakes in the Arizona sun at Pima County Air Museum. The faint traces of the gloss white paint can still be seen on the belly of this B-47E where it was painted to reflect radiation from thermo-nuclear blasts.

The
end of the line for hundreds of
B-52s was the bone yard at Davis
Monthan AFB, Arizona. This once
formidable force was gradually
reduced to scrap as part of the
Strategic Arms Limitation Treaty
agreement with the former Soviet
Union. This sea of aluminum was
photographed in April 1993.

seating, á la the B-47. Standard crew complement was six, with upward ejection seating for three and downward for two in the nose. The lonely tail gunner would leave the aircraft in an emergency by jettisoning the entire tail turret. This feature was eliminated with the development of the later B-52G in which the tail gunner joined the rest of the crew up front and operated the four-gun tail turret through remote control or the automatic fire control system.

The B-52 underwent a huge range of improvements as it entered service in numerous versions for varying roles. Although developed exclusively as a strategic, high-altitude nuclear bomber, it was later modified to operate as a low-level nuclear attack and later, a tactical bomber. These latter changes, which required extensive structural modification to the wing and center fuselage, bear testament to the flexibility of the original design. After outliving several intended replacements, including the fabulous but flawed North American XB-70 Mach 3 bomber,

the ultimate production variant became the B-52H. The aircraft shared the low-drag, short tail introduced with the G model, and its only distinguishing external feature was the Pratt & Whitney TF33-P-3 turbofans. These high bypass ratio engines (known as JT3D in civilian guise) were rated at 17,000 pounds thrust for the B-52H and, because they were mounted side by side in the same nacelle, required fan ducts to discharge through "banana nozzles" on their outboard side.

Of some 744 B-52s built, more than 90 were still in active service with the USAF by the late 1990s. Development problems with the Rockwell (later Boeing) B-1B Lancer and the huge costs associated with the Northrop Grumman B-2 Spirit stealth bomber, ensured the survival of the B-52. By 1997 the USAF was again considering a Boeing proposal to re-engine the bombers, this time with four Rolls-Royce RB.211-535E4 turbofans to be built in the United States by the British group's subsidiary, the Allison Engine Company.

The oldest B-52 still flying is owned by NASA and used for research flights at Edwards AFB, California. Officially designated as an NB-52B, its first notable role was as a launch platform for the North American X-15 rocket-propelled research aircraft. Note the all-important thick wing root and the four separate two-wheel landing gear trucks.

One of the first technical innovations to trickle "backwards" through the Boeing line was the turbofan engine. After its development for the 707, the 17,000-pound-thrust Pratt & Whitney TF-33 engine was adopted for the B-52H. It increased unrefueled range by 30 percent over the "G" model but required the design of a completely new double nacelle.

RIGHT
A meeting that many said would never happen. A Barksdale, Louisiana-based B-52H from the 410 Bomber Wing and visiting Russian Long-Range Aviation Tupolev Tu-95 Bear parked nose to nose at the Fairford International Air Tattoo. The Tu-95 grew from a Soviet copy of the B-29 and followed the same course of turboprop evolution as the B-52 until the U.S. bomber swapped to jets at the prompting of the USAF's Col. Pete Warden in 1948. The single 20-mm Vulcan multibarrel, radar-controlled cannon provided the B-52H with a potent sting in its tail.

OPPOSITE
The B-52H's 185-foot wingspan forms an impressive spectacle as the huge bomber runs in low with bomb doors open. The remaining fleet was equipped in the late 1990s to carry 12 AGM-86 cruise missiles externally and 8 internally. The nuclear-capable H fleet was also converted to assume the conventional weapons capability of the B-52Gs, which had been retired.

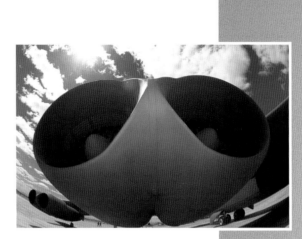

Pan American was the launch customer for the 707 and also launched the lengthened -300 intercontinental version. The -300 was initially powered by Pratt & Whitney's JT4A turbojet, but it wasn't until that was replaced with the new JT3D turbofan, as seen here, that sales took off. This particular aircraft, "Clipper Courser," was delivered to Pan Am in February 1964 and served the airline for 13 years before being sold. The "Intercontinental" also incorporated what amounted to a virtually new wing, with greater span, new leading- and trailing-edge flaps, and low-drag wing tips. *Boeing*

4
Classic Jetliners

The astounding success of the B-47 and the promise of the B-52 convinced many at Boeing that its real future lay with large military aircraft. Even when the British company deHavilland surprised much of the world in 1949 by flying a revolutionary jet-powered airliner, the DH-106 Comet, Boeing did not appear to be troubled—on the surface, at least. In marketing circles, however, it was a different story. "The Comet had a hell of an impact on Boeing's thinking. We had some people at the Farnborough air show who saw it demonstrated, and when they came home, they said, 'We'd better get into this business,'" said Joe Sutter.

The sleek British jet was a potential world beater and, along with another new jet venture from Avro Canada called the C-102, should have served as a dramatic wake-up call to Boeing and all its U.S. counterparts. Yet the military market was still the biggest target for Boeing and outwardly remained the focus for its design study efforts. However, the warning signs could not be ignored and even the Soviet Union's dabblings with the short- to medium-range Tupolev Tu-104 (a hasty civil conversion of the Tu-16 Badger bomber) convinced many at the company that its next effort should be aimed at both marketplaces.

In a sense, Boeing's future was about to be directed by the most fortunate serendipity in the history of aviation. In creating the USAF's front-line fast-jet bombers, it produced the requirement for a fast-jet tanker that would be capable of fueling the rapidly growing and exceedingly thirsty fleet. Obsolescent KC-97 tankers were simply not fast enough to keep pace with the B-47, which staggered dangerously close to its stall margin as the fuel was transferred and the load increased. Sure enough, in 1952 the USAF issued outline specifications for an aircraft with a 250,000-pound gross takeoff weight able to operate at the same speed and altitude as the new bombers. Out of this requirement was born the concept of a combined tanker/transport study that could provide an answer to both solutions.

Boeing's jet tanker/transport project was authorized by the board in May 1952, the same month as the Comet inaugurated the jet age of commercial aviation when it entered service with British Overseas Airways Corporation (BOAC). The (then) vast sum of $16 million of company money was allocated to the development of a prototype that was to be the basis for its bid to the USAF as well as the world's airlines. Boeing did not start the studies from scratch; the company's preliminary design unit had been working for longer than five years on studies of an improved Model 367/C-97 Stratofreighter. In fact, these long running efforts had reached the 80th study configuration by the time the project was authorized, so it was designated the 367-80. Research from another study, the Model 473-60C jet transport, also contributed to the outcome of the "Dash 80," as the project quickly became known.

The late decision to widen the cross-section to 148.5 inches, providing for six abreast in coach class, was the major selling point that helped it win the war against the DC-8 and established the basis for the jetliner dynasty.

The progenitor of more than 9,000 Boeing jetliners rests in the sunshine at Boeing Field in 1995. The pioneering Dash 80 is one of the most significant aircraft of all time and by 1990 was back in the care of Boeing. The company flew it back to Seattle from storage in Arizona on behalf of its owner, the Smithsonian Institution.

Although the design evolution of the entire jet transport family essentially began with the lumbering 367, it had already moved sufficiently far away from the original lines of the piston design that by the time "Dash 80" was conceived it bore few visible traces of its prop-driven ancestor. Early on in the process of design evolution, Boeing quickly recognized the benefits of incorporating as many features of the sleek new jet-powered designs as possible, a point recalled by George Schairer.

"About this time," Schairer said, "we had learned enough about using jet engines and about building big, fast airplanes that Maynard Pennell, in running the preliminary design unit, had got interested in the question: Could you build a good transport airplane using those same ideas? As I had pointed out, back in history, the B-17

and 307 used the same wings and tails; there was a different body. Could we do the same thing? Was there a way to take the wings of a B-47 or a -52 and the tails and put a body on which would make for a commercial transport?"

Ironically, the answer seemed to be a categorical no. "Well, the airlines didn't like it, didn't like any of the things we came up with," he recalled. "They didn't want the wing on the top of the body; they wanted the wing low on the body." Another problem was the bomber's bicycle landing gear, which took up space in the fuselage where the passengers should be. "There wasn't any way to move past the landing gears, and you needed passengers for nearly the full length of the airplane." The power requirement also posed problems. "We started our work that led to the 707 with two double pods. However, we had put the passen-

gers up over the wing, and we still had the landing gears up under the floor, but that was still a problem. It wasn't very good."

Once again for Boeing, the incongruous setting of a Dayton hotel room provided the right creative environment. "One weekend when we were busy working with the Air Force on the B-52 airplane, we took a few hours out and sketched away. We found out that we could mount the landing gear out on the wing and retract the landing gear sideways into the body. That was the start of our coming up with the final design of the 707," said Schairer.

The location of the tricycle gear was fundamental to the new design. In general, tricycle gears have to be close enough behind the center of gravity so that on takeoff the nose can still be raised with the main gear in contact with the runway. Yet the gear also has to be far enough back to prevent it tipping onto its tail during loading. By using a significant wing sweep angle, Boeing was able to pivot the main gear aft of the wing's rear spar. In the Comet, which had a relatively modest sweep angle of only 20 degrees, the gear had to be located forward of the rear spar. This meant

a hole had to be cut out of the wing's structural box to house the gear when retracted, thus reducing fuel carrying space and potentially compromising structural strength.

The folding movement of the main undercarriage required a short gear, which, in turn, meant the wing had to be close to the ground. But a low wing presented clearance problems for Boeing's popular pod-mounted engine configuration. The answer was to introduce dihedral (an upward sloped wing from root to tip) using design principles learned with the swept, though anhedral (downward sloping) configuration of the B-52. "We had learned from the B-52 that we could bend the wings up, so we kept the wings off the ground by raising them up. We had not known we could do that, but we found a breakthrough in the control system, so we could raise the wing tips up and lower the airplane closer to the ground." The cable runs to engines and control surfaces were located beneath the cabin floor and had fewer bends and pulleys than the more complex layout of the high-wing mounted bombers.

Although Boeing's background in bombers gave it an early lead, the company had problems "thinking" in terms of the broader commercial possibilities offered by the new jet

Designers learned major lessons in lateral control from mistakes made on the B-47. The combination of wing upper-surface spoilers and a small aileron behind the inboard nacelle on the 707 produced good lateral control at high speeds, avoiding the decrease in effectiveness of the outer aileron that had occurred on the B-47. The enhanced lateral control was equally vital for low speeds, where swept-wing aircraft had proved highly unstable in the past.

The 367-80 was soon hard at work with the USAF, proving its potential as a tanker. Demonstrations with an improved Boeing flying boom, seen here with a B-52 over the Puget Sound area in 1955, led to an initial order for KC-135A tanker/transports. *Boeing*

engines. The -80 fuselage, for example, was based on the same figure eight, "double-bubble" shape as the original 367, and even utilized the same 132-inch cabin width and 90-foot length. The double bubble was introduced to make the fuselage strong enough to be pressurized to hold sea-level conditions to 22,500 feet and yet light enough to be practical. It consisted of two circular arcs of different radii, with the larger one above forming the cabin faired into a smooth-contoured elipse using a concept pioneered on the Curtiss C-46.

The top section was designed for cargo and the lower deck for fuel tanks for B-52 refueling. However, even the USAF thought the design too small and an additional 12 inches were added to the cabin width to accommodate larger main deck cargo. The dimensions of the basic 367-80 prototype remained unchanged. Further changes followed as a result of competition with the Douglas DC-8.

On May 14, 1954, almost two years to the day after the project formally began, the yellow- and copper-colored -80 was rolled out of the Renton production site and into the morning sunlight for the first time. At this stage the term "707" was not widely adopted, even though the number assigned internally for the production version was in the 700 block from 1951 onwards. Boeing numbers up to 499 had been allocated to earlier aircraft, while 500 to 699 were reserved for industrial projects.

Years of refinement and more than 4,240 hours of wind-tunnel tests had generated an unfamiliar shape. Unlike the B-47 and B-52, the wing was below the fuselage and not on top, and the engines were hung in separate pods spaced out along the leading edge of the aerofoil. The main undercarriage consisted of two trucks, each with four wheels, that retracted inwards from the

An early model KC-135A Stratotanker with its original small vertical tail of the 707-120 and Pratt & Whitney J57P-59W turbojets. The noise-induced sonic fatigue from these engines proved so intense that the aft fuselage structure between the trailing edge and the USAF symbol required reinforcement with strengthening bands. *Boeing*

inboard wing rather than the fuselage. Few people at the time realized they were witnessing the emergence of a configuration that would dominate commercial jetliner design philosophy for the rest of the century. It was the first of a family of classic jetliners.

The wings were sharply raked back with a 35-degree sweep angle and arched upwards with a significant dihedral of 7 degrees. Large trailing edge flaps were divided to allow the high velocity jet blast to pass uninterrupted between them. Using the lessons of the B-47 and B-52, the wing was also fitted with both high- and low-speed roll control surfaces. A high-speed aileron, for use in the cruise, was located between the flap sections, with an outboard aileron situated near the wing tip for use during low-speed flight with flaps deployed. Roll control was augmented with spoilers which deployed differentially to act with the ailerons at high speeds or symmetrically to provide air braking. The spoilers made a dramatic difference on production versions. Roll rate without spoilers was a rather sluggish 10 degrees per second, compared to a more snappy rate of 30 degrees per second when they were operated alongside the ailerons. The -80 did not roll out with leading-edge flaps, though these were later added and appeared on production versions. Used for the first time on the 707, they hinged down from the leading edge to temporarily increase the camber of the wing for slow-speed flight. The approach speed of late production versions such as the 707-320B was subsequently as low as 110 knots (127 miles per hour) by use of the leading-edge flaps in combination with the trailing-edge Fowler flaps.

Flight control was achieved with aerodynamically balanced, manually operated small spring tabs on the trailing edge of each surface. This was a major decision, as many in the industry expected the new jet to be fitted with servo-hydraulic-powered controls. However the solution was simple, foolproof, and prevented the controls from being moved too quickly at high speeds. This was important because pressure mounted with increasing air speed. Furthermore, a recent discovery showed that dual hydraulic systems were needed as back-up in fighters, and Boeing had no experience with such systems. Trim tabs were normally used in piston airliners to control the pitch of the aircraft. The -80, however, used a system in which trimming was achieved by changing the angle of the entire horizontal stabilizer. Boeing had perfected the variable incidence tailplane with the B-52, marking the first use of such

a system on any large jet and made it controllable electrically with a manual back-up system.

The bogie undercarriage was another first for a Boeing commercial jetliner and would appear consistently on all subsequent large aircraft. Designed to withstand touchdown speeds up to 180 miles per hour, the tubeless tires on all 10 wheels contained enough rubber to make more than 100 automobile tires. The main wheels were pressurized to 180 pounds per square inch and took the impact of landing with the help of a Boeing-made oleo-pneumatic shock absorber with a travel of 22 inches, roughly 10 inches more than the piston-engined equivalent. For all its novelty, the gear caused one of the

A J57-powered C-135A owned by NASA takes off from Ellington Field, Houston, Texas, in 1997 on another zero g flight. The sight—and most notably the sound—of these early-build aircraft was becoming increasingly rare as KC-135s were either re-engined with high-bypass CFM56s or retired. As well as training astronauts, this "Vomit Comet," as the aircraft is named is also used for science missions and provided the filming environment for the movie *Apollo 13*.

A short-bodied 707-138, originally designed around a Qantas requirement, is pictured on takeoff. Boeing simply traded weight for fuel and extended the 707's range by chopping out a 10-foot section of fuselage aft of the wing. Today this rare bird, which first flew in March 1959, is used as a corporate transport.

first major upsets for the program when the left main unit collapsed during fast taxi trials and punched a jagged hole through the wing. Engineers discovered the design did not allow for structural deflections caused by the braking loads and that brittle steel in a fitting was partially to blame. The gear and wing were repaired and strengthened and Dash 80 finally took to the air for the first time on July 15, 1954.

Another design flaw in the gear also quickly revealed itself during flight testing when the brakes became too hot due to insufficient oil volume capacity and failed on one landing. Tex Johnston, the chief test pilot, had been forced to slew Dash 80 off the runway and into softer ground in an attempt to arrest the landing, resulting in the collapse of the nose gear leg.

The aircraft was designed around the P&W J-57 turbojet because this would provide optimum commonality between the B-52 and projected KC-135 tanker version, dubbed Model 717 by Boeing. As it did with the B-52 design, Boeing also clustered the engines in two twin pods. This was later dropped in favor of individual pods, which improved survivability in case of a catastrophic engine failure, as well as improving access for maintenance. Although turbofan engines were unknown to the design team at the time, it proved serendipitous when they became available, as the twin-pod nacelles would have required major redesign.

707 AND KC-135

Within days of the Dash 80's 1-hour and 24-minute-long maiden flight, it began evaluation flights for the USAF both as a transport and a tanker. For the latter role, the 367-80 was fitted with an improved version of the Boeing-built flying boom. The demonstrations were critical to the jetliner effort, as the company was counting on a military contract to defer development costs and provide the basis for subsequent commercial production with shared manufacturing jigs.

The demonstrations were also critical for other reasons. One thousand miles to the south Douglas was close to defining its own jet tanker/transport, the DC-8. The company had set up a project office in Santa Monica, California, in June 1952 to tackle exactly the same military and airline requirements as Boeing. Unlike the Seattle manufacturer, however, Douglas had a bulging order book for its commercial piston airliners, the DC-6B and DC-7, and was in no real hurry to get on with the DC-8. American Airlines, one of the key customers responsible for the development of the DC-7, had so much influence that it delayed Douglas' launching of the DC-8 for fear that it would sap engineering support for the big piston transport. Another factor influencing Douglas was the unfavorable early experience with jets it experienced with the development of the twin-engined XB-43 medium jet bomber. The XB-43 was used as a test bed for the General

New noise legislation introduced in the 1980s badly hit 707 operations. Middle East Airlines opted to keep flying by hush-kitting its aircraft with the "Super Q" conversion offered by Comtran International. Enlarged bypass duct collars reduced the 707's 100 EPNdB (noise decibel) footprint from 5.6 nautical miles to 2.8 nautical miles without affecting capabilities such as de-icing and thrust reversal. Just visible under the left wing is what appears to be a fifth engine. This is an engine ferry pod of the type first introduced with the -138 model.

Electric TG180 powerplant, and Douglas wrote up a list of 250 shortcomings of the engine as a result.

Yet despite Boeing's lead, Douglas was quietly confident that the U.S. government would stick to its "level playing field" aircraft procurement policy established from World War II onwards and buy batches of more than one aircraft type. In fact, neither Boeing nor Douglas was initially successful in the tanker contest. Lockheed's jet tanker design was selected as the winner around the time of the first flight of the Dash 80. However, to the consternation of both Douglas and Lockheed, the Dash 80 demonstration flights and the promise of early delivery dates forced a change of mind in the USAF, which simply went ahead and ordered 21 KC-135s in September 1954. The USAF did not place a single order for the Douglas jet and the "winning" Lockheed design never left the drawing board. The deal abruptly gave Boeing a leg up in the forthcoming commercial battle and effectively enabled the Seattle manufacturer to offset a good part of its initial investment. Furthermore, Boeing was able to price its civil 707s from ship 22 onwards, while Douglas was forced to mark up unit prices from ship 1.

The battle with Douglas was far from over, however, and competition with the DC-8 was to have a profound influence on the development of the 707 for years to come. One of the most crucial design drivers was the width of the cabin, which, as mentioned above, was already considered to be too narrow by even the USAF. When the first order for 20 707s was placed by Pan American on October 13, 1955, Boeing's joy was tempered by the news that the carrier had simultaneously ordered 25 DC-8s. One of the reasons for the larger Douglas order was the DC-8's wider 147-inch fuselage cross-section, a factor that also led to the loss of another order from United.

During negotiations with American Airlines, it therefore became obvious that if Boeing was to win this crucial order, the 707 cabin needed to be as wide, if not wider, than the DC-8's. But even at this stage the manufacturer was reluctant to alter the dimensions again, having already upped the cross-section to 144 inches for the USAF. A cornerstone of its program philosophy was maximum commonality between the KC-135 and 707, and the prospect of different manufacturing jigs was not popular. "The bean counters didn't want to change anything, but Douglas came along with the DC-8, and they did not have much choice. At a sales meeting with Ed Wells I said, 'Let's make it 1 inch wider than the DC-8.' Everybody knew we should build more comfort into the aircraft, and another inch would not kill it!" recalled Sutter. American ordered the 707 when the cross-section was ultimately widened to 148.5 inches, providing seating for six abreast in coach class.

When Pan American began commercial operations with the first production model on October 26, 1958, it was therefore with the wider fuselage specified by American. The first aircraft were designated 707-100 by the FAA-type certificate but 707-120 by Boeing, which developed a sequence in line with the designation -121 given to the first aircraft ordered by Pan Am. The number -21 was Boeing's customer code for Pan Am, American being -23, and TWA -31. The -100s were powered by 12,500-pound-thrust JT3C-6 turbojets, and most were re-engined with more efficient and more powerful (17,000–18,000-pound-thrust) JT3D turbofans later in life. Other than the wider and longer fuselage, the -100s differed from the

A_s commercial sales of the 707 tailed off, the government and executive transport business picked up. Here a 1976-vintage 707-300, owned since new by the State of Qatar, climbs out of London Heathrow on a late September evening in 1997.

Dash 80 in having a retractable Krueger leading-edge flap. The 12-foot-long flap was located between the engines and extended automatically when the trailing-edge flaps were lowered 9 1/2 degrees. Initial aircraft were also delivered with the same basic tail as the Dash 80, but further flight tests revealed directional stability issues, which were solved by increasing the height of the fin. A small ventral, or underfin, was also added to the bottom of the fuselage below the tail. This prevented pilots from "over-rotating" the 707 on takeoff, preventing an excessive nose-high attitude and loss of lift.

To cater to a special long-range requirement from Qantas, Boeing produced a "short-body" -100 version, designated the -138 after the Australian flag-carrier's customer code. To make the short body, a 10-foot plug was removed from the fuselage aft of the wing, giving it an overall length of 134 feet, 6 inches. This reduced structural weight but retained the same fuel load as the baseline aircraft, thereby increasing range. The original -100 series was therefore retrospectively designated the "long body." Although Qantas was the only customer for the short-body -100, buying 13 in total (including 6 turbofan -138Bs), it was a sure sign that Boeing was prepared to be flexible to meet airline requirements. For the first time it was matching the efforts of Douglas, which, as an old

hand at the airline game, was offering a wide range of DC-8 versions within a family. Boeing was about to grow a new "family" concept of its own.

Pratt & Whitney quickly came up with a more powerful turbojet, the JT4A, to combat the performance deficiencies that some operators experienced particularly at "hot and high" airfields. Boeing offered the -100 powered by the JT4A and called it the -200. For all Boeing's efforts, Braniff was the only customer; it ordered five for its South American services.

The big breakthrough for the 707, and the real beginning of Boeing's civil jetliner dynasty, came with the launch of the Intercontinental -300 Series. Known as the 707-320 by the manufacturer, the aircraft had genuine transatlantic capability, a longer fuselage, heavier weight, higher payload, greater fuel capacity, and more powerful engines. Of the 1,010 aircraft produced in the 707/720 series, some 580 were -300s, while a further 130 shared most of the larger aircraft's features.

The 707-320 made its first flight on January 11, 1959, and was in service with Pan Am by late July of that year. Initial aircraft were powered by the JT4A turbojet, but the emergence of the P&W JT3D turbofan transformed the performance of the 707 virtually overnight. The JT3D, which was available in different versions rang-

ing in thrust from 17,000 to 19,000 pounds, was such an improvement in terms of fuel efficiency, power, and lower noise that it was quickly offered for retrofit on the original -100s, which became known as -100Bs. Another version, the -400, was dimensionally identical to the -300 but was offered with the 16,500-pound-thrust Rolls-Royce Conway 505 and later the 17,500-pound-thrust Conway 508 engines. This was the first Boeing jetliner offered with a non-P&W engine option and the first to be powered by a commercial turbofan engine. The first of the 37 -400s built flew on May 20, 1959, followed by the first -300B in January 1962.

While the public spotlight was on the commercial 707 developments, the production of the KC-135 "Stra-totanker" provided Boeing with its real bread and butter income for the first decade of jetliner manufacturing. The differences between the two were significant enough for separate model numbers with the tanker/transport dubbed the 717. Not only was the tanker fuselage slightly narrower, but even the aluminum alloy used for the skin was different. In recognition of the different working life expected of the tanker, which would normally fly only one-tenth the time per year as that flown by the civil airliner, Boeing designed the tanker to a "safe-life" requirement. The more stressful, cyclical environment of the 707

demanded a "fail-safe" structure made of 2024 aluminum alloy, while the KC-135 could be adequately made from 7178 alloy.

In total, 820 KC-135 tanker/transports and C-135 "Stratolifter" transports were built at Boeing's Renton site. The vast majority, some 732 aircraft, were built as KC-135As, which were powered by the P&W J57P-53W turbojet, a 13,750-pound-thrust engine requiring water-injection for takeoffs at maximum gross weight. The last batch was completed with the newly available P&W TF33-P-5 turbofans, the military variant of the JT3D. With the gradual retirement of the commercial 707 fleets in the late 1970s and early 1980s, the vast supply of JT3D engines and larger, strengthened vertical tails were canni-balized from the older airliners and transferred to the KC-135 fleet. Many Air National Guard and USAF Reserve aircraft were retrofitted and designated KC-135E.

A more ambitious retrofit program involved re-engin-ing with the CFM56 high bypass ratio turbofan. Boeing had flight tested the new technology engine on a version of the 707 known as the -700. This was to have been the last new variant of the 707 offered for sale as well as for retrofit with the new engines but foundered among concerns that it would damage the market for the emerging 757. The single aircraft used for flight testing was ultimately

More
than 450 KC-135s have been given a
new lease on life by becoming re-
engined with the General
Electric/Snecma CFM56-2.
Compared with the basic KC-135A,
the KC-135R, as it is called, can
offload 65 percent more fuel at a
1,500-nautical-mile radius and up to
150 percent more fuel at a 2,500-
nautical-mile radius. Takeoff run is
also up to 2,500 feet shorter, and
noise footprint at 90 EPNdB is an
amazing 98 percent smaller.
Maximum takeoff weight also
increases by a dramatic 20,000
pounds, most of which is extra fuel.

The
last production 707 airframe, line
number 1012, was delivered to the
British Royal Air Force as the last of
six E-3D Sentry AEW Mk.1s. The most
distinctive feature of the E-3D is the
30-foot-diameter rotordome
containing the Westinghouse
AN/APY-1 surveillance radar. Like the
USAF, NATO, Saudi, and the French-
operated AWACS aircraft, the Sentry
uses its radar to guide interceptors
such as these RAF Panavia Tornado
F.Mk 3s to their targets.

reconverted back to use standard JT3Ds and sold to the
government of Morocco in April 1982, becoming the last
commercial 707 to be sold. The benefits of the new engine
were not lost on the USAF, however, which eagerly began
a program to re-engine as many KC-135s as it could. The
extra power and reduced fuel consumption of the CFM56
meant that up to 50 percent more fuel could be carried to
off-load to other aircraft. In all, the USAF predicted the
more efficient engines would save it $1.7 billion in fuel

bills over the first 15 years—or roughly enough to fill up
7.7 million cars every year over the same period. The
KC-135R program began in 1984, and by 1998 more
than 450 had been re-engined. Together with some avionics improvements and a comprehensive structural upgrade
effort, the provision of new engines ensures that KC-135s
will continue to be the mainstay of the USAF's tanker
force well into the twenty-first century.

BOEING 720

The inherent flexibility of the basic 707 design was
proven with the development of the 720, a medium-range
version produced by Boeing to compete with Convair's
CV-880, CV-990, and the DC-8 for domestic jet routes
within the United States.

The idea seemed simple at first. All Boeing had to do was
shrink the fuselage in much the same way as it had for the
707-138 version for Qantas and take some structural weight
out to help runway performance. Boeing initially offered the

aircraft as the 707-020, but probably due to its similarity with the short-body KC-135/717, it was changed to the 717-020. However, the designation caused too much confusion, so the aircraft finally emerged as the Boeing 720—up until the merger with McDonnell Douglas, the only member of the commercial jetliner family not to end with a number seven.

The 720 fuselage ended up 9 feet shorter than the -100, with an overall length of 136 feet, 2 inches. Significant weight reduction in areas like the undercarriage forgings and skin thicknesses pared the empty weight down to 110,800 pounds compared to 118,000 pounds for the baseline series 100 and 135,000 pounds for the larger intercontinental aircraft. The new version launched into production in November 1957, and United placed the first order (for 11) on December 17 that year. However, it was the competition for American Airlines' business that evoked the most design change in the aircraft.

American was very interested in the Convair CV-990, which was designed with high cruise speed as

Boeing test engineers prepare for another 720B sortie at Edwards AFB, California, on a cold morning in January 1961 during FAA certification tests at speeds up to Mach 0.9. The major external change to the shorter-bodied 720 was the revised wing. The leading-edge sweep between the inboard nacelles and the fuselage was increased, and Krueger leading-edge flaps, seen clearly in this picture, were installed for almost the full span. *Boeing*

The availability of the Pratt & Whitney JT3D turbofan transformed the 720 just as it did the 707. The 720B, as the JT3D version was called, was able to cruise 21 miles per hour faster, to 622 miles per hour, and climb faster. Ceiling was also boosted almost 2,000 feet to 40,000 feet. *Boeing*

the top priority. An innovative fan bypass engine from General Electric, the CJ805-21, was earmarked for the aircraft and promised good performance. Worse still for Boeing, Convair had successfully sold the CV-990 to Capitol Airlines, and American was convinced that its competition would use the high-speed characteristics of the Convair to great advantage in the war for passengers. Two important developments emerged as a result: the P&W JT3D turbofan and a high-speed wing for the 707/720 models.

Pratt & Whitney had moved onto the higher thrust JT4D turbojet when the turbofan concepts emerged first from Rolls-Royce in the form of the Conway and secondly from GE with the CJ805-21. It had publicly played down any perceived benefits but privately maintained some study work. It was therefore quick to present performance estimates of a turbofan version of the JT3, which would have a bypass ratio of 1.5. Although not as great as the 2.2 ratio of the GE engine, or as far advanced as the relatively modest 0.3 bypass ratio of the Conway, the P&W engine had the solid installed base of the JT3/JT4 behind it and huge support from Boeing. The JT3D went on to become the standard powerplant for the 707, as well as the bulk of the 154 720s built.

The high-speed wing development was another story. "American was wheeling and dealing with Convair, which had developed 'speed bumps' [or Whitcomb fairings as they were sometimes called, after the discoverer of the area rule] for their aircraft. Now, although Boeing didn't think the market looked that huge, we still thought we'd better do something about it because American was a very important customer. So we looked at fine tuning the wing to see if we could increase Mach cruise speed to match the Convair," said Joe Sutter. "I

argued strongly that if we didn't get the speed up, Convair would win the deal. I was also sure we could increase speed without changing the whole wing, which would have been too expensive. We thought we had enough basic knowledge to commit to it.

"The Mach critical speed was defined by the inboard wing panel, which is where we concentrated our work. We developed this fiberglass glove to put over the existing wing, which moved the contour of the leading edge forward. This had the effect of moving the center of pressure forward at the root section while maintaining the same effective sweep angle. It basically kept the whole of the wing 'critical' at the same time," recalled Sutter. Viewed from above, the glove altered the sweep of the leading edge between the inboard engine and the fuselage to produce double taper. "We got an increase of 0.02 Mach out of it, which was lucky because that's what we guaranteed to American!" The modified wing design was also adapted for the turbofan-powered 707-120B, increasing wing area from 2,433 square feet to 2,521 square feet, although -100s converted to the new engines were not fitted with the revised wing.

In the end, American bought both the CV-990 and 720B, though the Convair fleet was long outlived in service by the Boeing fleet, which was called "707-Astrojets" to avoid causing confusion for its passengers who were by then also flying on its fleet of 707-123s. Despite the innovations of the engine and wing, which was also fitted with Krueger leading-edge flaps along almost the entire span for improved short-field performance, the 720 was not a huge success, and the last was delivered in September 1967. The good news for Boeing, however, was that it was eclipsed by another Renton product that was itself destined to break the record books—the 727.

Fate was not kind to the 720, which was quickly overtaken by the 727-200. Only 154 were built, one of the last to survive being this ex-MEA 720 seen in storage at Mojave Airport, California, in late 1996. Note the double taper of the leading edge.

The oval-shaped, number two tail-engine intake disturbed flow into the engine and caused it to surge on the first flight of the 727. Vortex generators, like those visible on the fin, were placed inside the S-duct to solve the problem. This ex-American Airlines 727-23 is seen at London Gatwick in the colors of Baltic International Airlines

5
Trijets and Twinjets

The 727 is possibly the most unusual design produced by Boeing. It is the only trijet, the only jetliner in the "7-series" family with a "clean" wing and the first—and probably last Seattle design—to be configured with a high "T-tail." As the first all-new member of the jetliner family, it also represents the first significant building block of the "family" concept that was to ensure Boeing's dominance in years to come. Yet why did it emerge looking so different from the 707 and other predecessors, and what, if anything, did it share with those earlier designs?

Encouraged by growing passenger acceptance of jet power in the late 1950s, Boeing foresaw the need for an economical short- to medium-haul jetliner that would make money on domestic routes where the four-engined alternatives, including the 720, would be too large and inefficient.

Studies began in 1956 and covered everything from twinjets to four-engined mini-airliners. Two of the key potential launch customers, Eastern Airlines and United Airlines, tugged Boeing in two directions. Eastern wanted a twin for low cost, while United preferred a four-engined design that could cope with the demands of high-altitude operations from its 5,000-foot base in Denver, Colorado.

The 727, as the effort was called, graduated to project status by September 1959 when Boeing had finally persuaded the airlines to compromise on a three-engined aircraft that would use the existing fuselage cross-section of the 707. The

hallmark of the 727, and the chief design goal, was the ability to operate into and out of shorter runways than any other jetliner. This would open up a huge number of regional and provincial airfields, enabling the 727 to tap the routes dominated by prop-driven aircraft.

"The big change with the 727 was the swing to short-haul operations," recalled Joe Sutter. "We designed its performance around places like La Guardia, New York, and Washington D.C.'s National, which only had runways of around 5,400 feet in length at the time. The main effort was aimed at reorienting the wing design with a powerful set of high-lift devices. This was therefore the first Boeing to have slats on the leading edge of the wing and triple slotted flaps." The prime benefit of jet power, namely speed, was not forgotten, however, and the same wing was required to operate at a maximum speed of Mach 0.9. "The high speed was achieved by basically tuning up on the aerofoil work we'd done for the 707/720," added Sutter.

The need to get the most out of the wing helped push the design toward a configuration with all three engines clustered around the tail. By putting all the powerplants around the tail, the wing was left uncluttered, or "clean" and could be configured with unrestricted high-lift devices. By grouping the engines close together, the problems of asymmetric thrust in the case of engine failure were also

A distinctive design feature of the 737, retained throughout all its revisions, is the uncovered main undercarriage wheels. The use of undercarriage doors was considered unnecessary, and wind-tunnel tests proved their omission had virtually no measurable effect on drag.

The first 727 is preserved at the Seattle Museum of Flight's restoration site at Paine Field, Everett, Washington. The old trijet first flew in February 1963 and clocked 64,492 hours and 48,057 takeoffs and landings, carrying more than 3 million passengers for its owner, United Airlines. Note the relative size of the 727, a short- to medium-haul airliner, against the diminutive deHavilland Comet—the world's first jetliner. The difference is even more surprising given that the preserved example is a Comet 4C—the final stretch version of the Comet series!

minimized. The cabin was also quieter. The alternative tri-jet layout with one engine hung in a pod below each wing and the third engine in the tail (similar to the Lockheed L-1011) was finally dropped by the time the 727 got the internal go-ahead in August 1960.

The tail-mounted engine concept originated in commercial aviation with the design of the Caravelle by the French company Sud-Aviation. The idea of installing a third engine in the tail had been pioneered by Martin with the XB-51 design in 1948. Boeing studied a mid-tail horizontal stabilizer like the Caravelle but finally followed the high "T-tail" design adopted by the very similar deHavilland DH-121 Trident. The British Trident design, although very similar to the 727, was heavily tailored to the needs of British European Airways, whereas the Boeing jetliner was built around the varying requirements of four major U.S. trunk carriers.

The two aircraft almost shared the same engine at an early stage when Rolls-Royce was Boeing's choice to power the 727 with an Allison-built variant of what eventually evolved into the Spey. However, launch customer Eastern Airlines, led by the ebullient Eddie Rickenbacker, pushed for a more powerful Pratt & Whitney engine. The U.S.

powerplant maker responded by offering to develop an engine specially for the 727. This was to be based on the two-shaft J52 turbojet already designed under a U.S. Navy Bureau of Weapons contract to power the Grumman A-6 Intruder. The engine was called the JT8D and was originally designed to produce 13,200 pounds of thrust for the new trijet. In its initial -9 version for the 727, however, it generated a thrust of 14,500 pounds. The basic simplicity and robustness of the design made it into the most popular civil jet engine in the world with more than 14,000 built. The JT8D later grew into a large family of jets powering big sellers like the 737, the Douglas DC-9, and, of course, the 727.

Boeing's fixation with the low-speed performance of the 727 resulted in some serious studies of a blown flap system, which was tested on the Dash 80. "To achieve the coefficient of lift that we wanted, we looked hard at a blown flap system," said Sutter. "In fact, the program people were so serious about it that they shut down the rest of the development for six weeks at one stage so we could concentrate on it." In the end, the system was rejected in favor of more conventional—but highly sophisticated—triple-slotted flaps. "We could have made it work, and, in

fact, it worked well on the Dash 80, but you had to have bleed air from the engines and lots of ducting," he said. The triple-flap arrangement, which cunningly folded up into the relatively compact wing when stowed, was the product of a "tremendous amount of Boeing research and development," Sutter added. The lessons learned played a valuable part in flap designs of several later models including the 737, 747, and 757.

One of the concerns about the design was the proximity of the wing's trailing edge to the side-mounted engine inlet. The venerable Dash 80 was again wheeled out to prove the design, and the prototype JT8D was bolted to the aft port side of the aircraft and flown to see if downwash and wake from the wing affected engine operability. The wing itself was also fitted with scaled-up flaps and leading-edge devices to try to duplicate flow con-

ditions from the 727 wing. Lew Wallick, Boeing test pilot for the first flight of the 727, recalled the Dash 80 testing. "We did stalls up to 35,000 feet; we did stalls at low altitude; we went reasonably fast with it, did sideslips, accelerations, decelerations, and eventually had a reverser that we used and did tests on the runway using reverse thrust, and that engine always behaved beautifully."

One particularly disturbing effect of the configuration on the center, number two engine was revealed at the worst possible moment—the 727's maiden flight. In perfect weather, on February 9, 1963, the first 727 accelerated down the runway at Renton toward Lake Washington at the north end of the field. "Everything was normal, and just about the time we got to the very end of the runway, all you could see was water and Mercer Island out ahead. It was terrible, terrible, two loud engine surges," said Wal-

Until
the advent of aerodynamic modification packages, only two options remained for future 727 operators: hush-kitting or re-engining. UPS chose the latter and with Dee Howard of Texas developed the 727QF, or "Quiet Freighter." The modification involved development of a larger S-duct to meet the higher airflow requirements of the Stage 3-compatible Rolls-Royce Tay 651 turbofans, which replaced the original JT8Ds.

lick. "We immediately throttled back a little bit and kept climbing, and I think we got to about 15,000 feet before we touched the throttles again. It turned my hair white."

The unexpected surge events, in which the flow of pressurized air within part of the engine is momentarily reversed, were caused by the distortion of airflow down the serpentine S-duct in the tail. The funneling effect caused instability in the flow as the aircraft rotated for takeoff, causing the surges. To Boeing's relief, the problem was simply solved by ringing the intake duct with vortex generators similar to those first used on the wing of the B-47. The small devices swirled the flow to prevent stagnation along the sides of the duct and promoted smooth flow into the engine. The later 727-200 models had circular intakes in the number two engine rather than the oval intakes on the first generation. Despite the fix, the early JT8D performance in flight test continued to be disappointing, however, and some, like Jack Steiner, occasionally wished that Rolls-Royce was still in the game. "The JT8D was pulled out of the hat at the last second," he said. "It wasn't a good engine at all. We could destroy it by making it surge, and it simply would destroy itself."

The first flight also revealed problems with the leading-edge devices, which could not be retracted for the whole flight. Stronger actuators were needed for the four leading-edge slats on each outer section and three Krueger flaps on the inboard section. Together with the trailing-edge flaps, the leading-edge devices contributed to a 25-percent increase in area to the 1,700-square-foot-area wing when deployed.

Flight testing did reveal some pleasant surprises, however, including the aircraft's excellent handling qualities. This was largely attributed to the dual hydraulically powered flight control system, which was a step beyond that of the 707. Roll control was achieved with inboard and outboard ailerons as well as spoilers. The outboard ailerons were fitted with balance tabs while all four ailerons were fitted with control tabs. Each wing had seven spoilers, five of which could be activated in flight to act as either flight control surfaces or air brakes. Two inboard sections on each wing acted as brakes on the ground only.

Pitch control was achieved with a dual-powered variable incidence tailplane, which, like the flight control system, was fitted with direct manual reversion. The elevators were also controlled hydraulically by dual systems with control tab manual reversion. The 727 was also the first of the family to feature a dual, or split, rudder. Each rudder was controllable using dual hydraulic power with a back-up third system for the lower rudder.

So much attention was paid to the flight control system because of the danger of "deep stall" that was inherent in the T-tail design. Boeing was well aware of the danger, having seen the British experience problems with two T-tail airliners, the BAC (British Aircraft Corporation) One Eleven and DH-121 Trident. The problem occurred when the wake from the wing effectively blanked off the airflow over the upraised elevator, rendering the flight control surface useless as a means of pushing the nose down and recovering from the stall. Boeing test pilot Dick Loesch recalled, "We had similar trouble, but our airplane recovered from stalls. I think that we only got into a stall twice. The airplane was loaded in a very adverse way, but still recovered."

Either way the effect of so much in-built safety backup and sophistication made aircraft handling a treat, according to Loesch. "It was so distinctly different from the 707s and Dash 80, and so much better. It was just night and day as far as I'm concerned," he said. Wallick added, "It was one of the first airplanes that was truly a one-hand airplane. You didn't have to muscle it around. It was kind of like a sports car in those days. It set a standard in flying qualities that Boeing followed." In one test demonstration to a pilot who had been used to flying piston transports, the Boeing pilot Brian Wygle turned off both hydraulic systems to show him manual reversion. Having warned him that the "last-ditch device was really a miserable way to fly the airplane," the pilot flew along for a while, and said it was "just like a DC-6."

Another major advance on the 727, and one that was to become a foundation for the future, was the autopilot and autoland system. The aircraft was fitted with dual FD110 flight director systems, a single-channel autopilot, dual vertical gyros, dual yaw dampers, and a performance data system. "Even on the very initial part of the airplane's test program, we had an autopilot that would fly the airplane right down to the runway, even though at that time we didn't have autoland. We could bring it down to 30 to 40 feet above the runway, disconnect, and land. Very successful!" recalled Wallick.

Another first for the aircraft was the provision of an onboard, self-contained auxiliary power unit, or APU. The need for an APU reflected the more austere conditions that Boeing expected the 727 would find itself in as it strayed further from the major international airports deep into propeller territory. The Garrett AiResearch (now AlliedSig-

nal) GTC85 APU was buried in the wing center section between the wheelwells and provided electrical power and compressed air for engine starting and air conditioning on the ground. This reduced its reliability on ground-based power carts and other amenities at airports, which sometimes were poorly equipped for jets.

By the time of the first flight in 1963 the order book stood at a healthy 131 from eight customers. Almost immediately Boeing began a series of improvements following the pattern established with the 707. Higher takeoff weights, cargo, and quick change variants became available as engine power increased and early reliability problems were overcome. The biggest and most important change came in August 1965, when the company announced the go-ahead of a stretched 727. The new version, dubbed the -200, was a simple extension over what was now called the -100 series and was stretched with two 10-foot plugs either side of the wing. Initially the -200 had the same fuel capacity and gross weight as the heaviest -100s and flew for the first time on July 27, 1967.

As with the -100, the -200 experienced rapid growth in max takeoff weight as more powerful JT8D engines became available. Weight grew to 170,000 pounds as the JT8D-11s and -15s were offered with ratings of 15,000 pounds and 15,500 pounds thrust, respectively. However, most operators wanted more range to go with the higher capacity of the stretch, and the initial -200s simply did not have the required legs. The last major 727 variant to be developed, and the one that gave the single largest boost to the order book, was the Series 200 Advanced. Introduced

Amazingly, Boeing developed and had approved a JATO modification for Mexicana 727-264s to enable them to operate at heavy weights from hot and high airports in the region. This solution would not go down too well in the current era of environmental sensitivity! *Boeing*

in 1970, the Advanced again featured higher gross weights (eventually reaching 209,500 pounds) but this time incorporated increased fuel capacity. It also had a cleverly redesigned interior to give a "widebody" look and used more powerful JT8D-17R engines capable of up to 16,400 pounds thrust. By September 1972 the trijet order book reached the magic 1,000 mark. Delta took delivery of this aircraft, a Series 200 Advanced, in January 1974.

Further growth studies continued in the 1970s in close association with airlines like United, which almost launched a Series 300. This was a further stretch of 18 feet, 4 inches to produce comfortable seating for around 180 in the standard six-abreast fuselage. However, time and technology were catching up on the 727, and the proposed -300 was abandoned when serious studies of an all-new 7N7 began. In late 1982, production of the 727 wound down as its successor, the 757, began to take shape. The last of 1,831 aircraft produced during the life of the program was a -200F Advanced for Federal Express, which was delivered on September 18, 1984.

The 727 had exceeded all expectations both in terms of sales and actual performance and established a new benchmark for Boeing. Importantly, it was a profitable program during the 1970s when Boeing was struggling to overcome huge debts from the launch of the 747, losses on the 737, and the overall effects of the oil crisis. Despite its vintage, the 727 remained an attractive passenger aircraft well into the late 1990s. This was particularly true of the -200 Advanced, which accounted for more than half of all the trijets built. Some freighter versions, equipped with hushkits or re-engined with the Rolls-Royce Tay 651-54 by United Parcel Service, are expected to remain in service until around 2020.

FAT ALBERT—THE 737

The development story of the 737 is nothing short of amazing. Almost canceled twice, the 737 family eventually blossomed into the best-selling jetliner in history and by 1999 was in the process of expanding to include a record ninth major variant.

The story begins in 1962 when Boeing began its first studies into the short-haul regional jetliner market. By 1964 these had become more serious because of growing competition in the shape of the British-built BAC One Eleven and Douglas DC-9. For the first time Boeing saw itself becoming forced into a defensive marketing move to reduce the penetration of the newcomers into the lower

end of the 727 market. But by late 1964 the competition was well ahead. The DC-9 had amassed more than 230 orders, and the similarly configured BAC One Eleven was well into flight tests in England and had already won a major order from American Airlines.

It was therefore somewhat of a gamble for the Boeing board when it gave the program the tentative go-ahead in November 1964. The initial configuration was built around an 85-seater with a 500-nautical-mile range and excellent short-field performance. In the early stages it had tail-mounted engines and a T-tail and looked more like the DC-9 than the 737 design that ultimately emerged. Boeing's thinking was heavily influenced by the other configurations of the day, which had, in turn, been inspired by the French Caravelle. "Douglas sort of accepted tail-engined configurations as a way of producing the best design for smaller jetliners and came up with the DC-9," said Joe Sutter. "We laid out our design and ended up with a sort of DC-9 ourselves."

The phenomenon of deep stall, although effectively designed out of the similarly T-tailed 727, still nagged at the configuration team. "Frankly, I was looking at this thing, and deep stall was a consideration. I went to my office and took out a three-view drawing and cut the engines out and started putting them in different locations. I felt we could put the [engine] barrel under the wing and get the turbine out behind the rear spar," said Sutter.

"Red" and "Blue" teams studied the low-engine and tail-engine designs and came up with surprising results. For identically sized aircraft the under-wing engine-mounted design yielded an extra six passenger seats. Sutter, who together with Jack Steiner, received the patent on the 737 design, says that as a result of the studies, he was "the guy that caused them to put the engines under the wing where they belonged." Another key difference from the DC-9 that helped sway the design change was the width of the 707-based fuselage. "We had a wider cross-section, as opposed to the DC-9, but if we'd put engines on the back end of that fuselage, the aerodynamic effects would have been horrendous," he added.

The wing was one of the original features to survive the scrutiny of both Red and Blue teams. "It had only modest sweep (25 degrees at quarter chord) and was built for excellent takeoff and landing performance. We placed huge emphasis on that," said Sutter. Another feature that was to have long-term repercussions was the decision to increase the dihedral of the main wing spars

The 727's sophisticated high-lift devices are nicely lit up in this photograph of a Sun Country -200 lifting off from Las Vegas McCarran International on a spring evening in 1993.

Large operators of the popular -200 Advanced aircraft, such as American, prolonged the life of their fleets either by hush-kitting or aerodynamic modification packages developed by companies such as Raisbeck.

The retractable leading-edge slats outboard of the taper break, inboard Krueger flaps, and triple-slotted flaps are well illustrated in this view of a Delta Airlines 727-232 powering out of Dallas-Fort Worth.

The rare sight of a 737-100. Only 30 models of this short-bodied "baby" jetliner were built before production was wholly turned over to the 6-foot-longer -200 Series. This was one of 22 originally ordered by launch customer Lufthansa and is seen here in the colors of Continental.

outboard of the engine mount. The wing emerged from the root with a 6-degree dihedral but canted up even farther beyond the engine, increasing the depth of the aerofoil. "That's the first Boeing airplane to have both spars cranked, and of course, it gave us a fuel capacity which is still favoring the airplane," said Jack Steiner. "I actually doubt that the airplane would be as successful as the new ones are today if we didn't have that added fuel capacity. We've got a lot of fuel capacity in that bird for the span."

The wing design was not perfect, however, and required numerous modifications to reduce drag and improve performance. Worse still, the first wing failed in a jig under a structural test at less than 100 percent of design load. This meant the production wing had to be strengthened, which added more weight.

The close proximity of the stubby jet's wing to the ground prevented the use of the pylons or struts like those of the 707 or 727, so an outboard installation similar to that of the B-47 was adapted for the 737. The original B-47 "string-tube" nacelle concept was also initially adopted for the JT8D, but this proved unsuccessful and was replaced by a revised design. To maximize the cost-saving benefits of commonality, the 737 engine was also designed to use the same cascade thrust reverser as the 727, but this also proved almost useless in early tests. Despite the enormous $24 million redesign costs involved, good landing performance was an absolute requirement, and the device was replaced with a Rohr-designed bucket-type reverser based on that of the DC-9. To save additional weight and complexity, the design team decided to leave off gear doors so the wheels were exposed in the bays when stowed.

Although the design, therefore, began to diverge away from the 727, it retained 60-percent parts commonality with the trijet and the 707, particularly in the cabin and flight deck areas. Other 727-derived features included dual hydraulic-powered ailerons with manual reversion, leading-edge slats and Krueger flaps, and dual hydraulic-powered elevator and rudder. Like the 707, it also had a variable-incidence tailplane trim system driven by dual electric-drive motors with manual backup. In common with its larger relatives, the 737 was also equipped with spoilers to assist with lateral control as well as braking. In systems technology the little jet also followed the lead of the 727 in using the same Garrett AirResearch GTC85 APU, though this time it was located in the tail. This was the favored location for the APU in every Boeing jetliner from the 737 onwards.

As the design crystallized, it became clear that the lead candidate to launch the 737 was the German flag carrier Lufthansa, though all the early betting had been on United. The European airline was searching for a jet to replace its prop fleet of Convair 240s and Vickers Viscount aircraft, and it was enthusiastic about the small Boeing despite overtures from BAC and Douglas. In last-minute negotiations, Lufthansa persuaded Boeing to grow the aircraft slightly to seat 100 to make it more competitive with the DC-9. Boeing agreed, and Lufthansa launched the 737-100 with an order for 22 in February 1965, making the new twinjet the first of the family to be launched by a non-U.S. operator.

Recalling its sales campaigns against the DC-8, when flexibility had been the key to victory, Boeing once again listened hard to its customers and almost immediately agreed to build another, slightly longer version to win the United order. In April 1965 the U.S. carrier, a long-time Douglas loyalist, turned its back on the DC-9 and ordered 40 stretched aircraft, now called the 737-200. It seemed as if Boeing was onto another winner, and by the time it delivered the first aircraft to Lufthansa in December 1967, the company had orders for 185 from 19 airlines in 10 countries.

The -200 was stretched by 6 feet, 6 inches over the -100, giving it an overall length of just over 100 feet and

Designers studied various configurations before adopting the final 737 design. The T-tail variant nearest the camera closely resembles the DC-9, which the 737 was launched to compete with. Ironically, it also resembles the MD-95 regional jet, which was renamed the 717 in January 1998 following the Boeing takeover of McDonnell Douglas (see chapter 8).

room for up to 130 coach-class passengers. Wingspan and all other dimensions remained otherwise unchanged. The longer 737 used the more powerful 16,000-pound-thrust JT8D-9, -15, or -17 engine in new "quiet" nacelles for noise reduction. Like virtually every Boeing product before it, the popularity of the original short-body -100 quickly waned with the availability of the larger variant. In the end, only 30 -100s were produced up until late 1969, including the development aircraft, which was sold to NASA as a test bed in 1973. This aircraft (N73700) was retired to Seattle's Museum of Flight in 1997. The -200, on the other hand, continued to be developed into ever more capable versions as engine power increased and other aerodynamic and systems improvements were introduced. In May 1971 this process culminated with the development of the 737 Series 200 Advanced.

The new features of the Advanced 737 included a wide series of mostly aerodynamic improvements. These were concentrated around the wing, which featured a thickened engine strut, a minor repositioning of the slats and a smoothing of the leading edge that was exposed behind them when deployed. Other

Development
of the 737-200 Advanced
dramatically improved the fortunes
of the twinjet, just as the similar
200ADV initiative had boosted sales
of the 727. Changes included
aerodynamic improvements to the
engine strut and exposed leading
edge underneath the slats as well as
an extension of the inboard Krueger
flap. This area is clearly seen in this
spectacular view of a Southwest
Airlines aircraft taking off from its
Dallas, Love Field base.

Concern
over the possible ingestion of debris
into the low-hanging jet intakes led
to the development of "Gravel Kits"
for aircraft that were intended to
operate from unprepared strips. Part
of the kit was a "vortex dissipater"
that bled engine air pressure and
blew it down through a small tube
projecting forward from the base of
each engine nacelle. The air blast
was directed forward to break up
ground vortices that would have
sucked up debris into the engine.

changes included an increase in droop of two slat sections, the extension of the Krueger flaps inboard, a sealing of the gap between spoilers and flaps, and the addition of a new automatic braking system. A total of 249 non-Advanced 737-200s were built until production shifted to the new model, and retrofit kits were made available to operators of early aircraft. The Advanced model sold well and helped sales of the 737-200 reach 1,114 by the time deliveries were completed in August 1988.

For several years in its early life, the program labored under the threat of cancellation. Its birth had been difficult to begin with, not so much because of the aircraft itself, but due, instead, to the timing of its development. The 737 competed for resources with the 727-200 and 747. The most important of these resources were human, and the 737 suffered because of a dilution in skills as engineers and mechanics were assigned to help the 747 in particular.

The unusual "portable" production jigs used to make the first 737s also made it vulnerable to cancellation rather than increasing its survivability, as might be supposed. The original site of the production line was at Boeing Field, and it was only moved to its current site at nearby Renton in late 1970. "It's the only movable wing tooling Boeing has ever had, as far as I know," said Steiner. "It was made movable so we could move the whole thing to Wichita [where 737 fuselages have been made since the start of the program]. Later on I had the job of bringing it from its station south of Plant 2 over to Renton." However, the transportability of the jigs also tempted Boeing to sell the program. "We used it another time that has never really been talked about, and that is during the crunch [1970]," Steiner continued. "We offered the whole caboodle to the Japanese. We were dead serious about trying to get money from anything. I can't tell you that we would have gone through with it, but the intention was there. We were broke."

The same financial crisis had an impact on orders, which plummeted dramatically. In 1973 a task force was formed to examine whether the 737 should be continued, as deliveries had dived from a peak of 114 in 1969 to just 22 in 1972, and only 14 had been ordered that year. Although only 23 were delivered in 1973, the development of the Advanced, plus a gradual market recovery, prompted a steady build-up in orders and, thankfully for Boeing, the 737 was not axed.

737-300/400/500

The mid-1970s was a period of intense debate within Boeing. It had produced some best-selling products, yet it could not afford to ignore the march of technology. This was evident in several areas, chief of which was propulsion. The new high-bypass turbofan engines under development at the time promised big fuel savings as well as low noise, two big incentives in an industry still recovering from the shock of successive oil crises and facing the new onslaught of stiff environmental rules.

The big question was should it embrace the new technology and upgrade its existing aircraft, or should it start with a clean-sheet design? The answer for the 727, after some debate, was the new design that led to the birth of the 757. The solution for the 737, on the other hand, was a substantial upgrade, with new engines, a modern flight deck, revised systems, and refined aerodynamics. So dramatic were the changes, in fact, that the new-look 737 was in essence a new aircraft. Yet it was the inherent strength of the original design and the positioning of the engines beneath the wings rather than at the tail that allowed the new developments to take place.

In January 1979 Boeing made its decision to stick with the existing 737 as the basis for its new development efforts in the 100- to 150-seat, short- to medium-range market. At the Farnborough air show in September 1980 the company made its first public reference to a new series, the 737-300, and was holding intense negotiations with the two main engine candidates: CFM International with

Like its trijet sisters, the 737 was penalized because of its noisy engines. Sabena reacted by hush-kitting its fleet as clearly indicated by the revised intake, longer nacelle, and new mixer/ejector at the rear of the engine.

the CFM56 and Rolls-Royce with its proposed RJ500. The base-line configuration was established within five months, and in March 1981 the program was formally launched when Boeing announced orders from Southwest Airlines and USAir for 10 each plus additional options. All were CFM56-powered.

One glance at the 737-300 revealed the adaptability of the basic design. The fatter, higher bypass ratio CFM56 engines could not be hung below the wing like the original JT8Ds and so, instead, were cantilevered out ahead of the wing's leading edge. This emphasized the true benefit of the 1960s decision to locate the engines close to the center of gravity rather than at the tail, which would have meant far more radical changes to adapt to the larger engines. The issue of ground clearance still presented a challenge, however, so the lower section of the nacelle was slightly flattened. Much to CFM International's and Boeing's surprise, the performance of the engine was actually marginally improved by the odd-looking intake lip. Some 15 years later the same basic inlet shape was used by Boeing for the design of the variable area engine intake on its Joint Strike Fighter proposal.

The added power of the 22,000-pound-thrust CFM56 meant Boeing could introduce the first major

stretch of the 737 since the initial jump to the -200 Series. One 3-foot, 8-inch plug was inserted forward of the wing and another 5-foot plug was sandwiched between the wing, root and the tail. The cabin length was increased to 77 feet, 2 inches as a result, providing seating for up to 149, while overall length rose to 109 feet, 7 inches. Increased power and length also meant more changes to the span of the wings and tailplane, as well as to the vertical tail, which was increased in area with a new dorsal fin and equipped with more powerful rudder actuation and yaw damper devices. The span increased to 94 feet, 9 inches, while the tailplane grew to 41 feet, 8 inches.

Despite the obvious logic of the 737-300 development, Boeing still studied all-new 150-seat designs in the early 1980s. By the winter of 1982–83 it was discussing a vague design called the 7-7 that gradually evolved into a 757 derivative, powered by IAE V2500s. Two years later the 7-7 concept had evolved again into the advanced 7J7, a high-tech airliner with fly-by-wire flight controls and propfan engines that would have been developed with Japan. While all these studies were taking place, the concept of a further 737 stretch, the -400, was slowly taking root. By 1985 airline interest was pushing Boeing into action, and the -400 was "pre-implemented" for launch in

the last few months of that year. The 7J7 was still very much alive at the time, and Boeing characterized the -400 as a sort of stop-gap aircraft until the high-tech propfan became available around 1992. However, the 7J7 was later indefinitely postponed, and the 737-400 emerged victorious with a launch order for 25 from Piedmont Airlines on June 4, 1986.

The -400 was the ultimate in "simple stretches" and was essentially little more than a -300 with a 120-inch fuselage extension. The two fuselage plugs, one of 48 inches aft and the other of 72 inches forward, produced an aircraft that was just 5 inches shorter than the original Dash 80. Furthermore, the Boeing "baby" had now grown to accommodate up to 171 in all-economy, just 3 fewer than a similarly configured 707-120! Wings, systems, and flight deck,

which had been updated with a modern two-crew digital avionics suite on the -300, were essentially identical to the preceding stretch. Other than local strengthening to cope with the higher operating weights of up to 150,000 pounds, the two aircraft were basically identical.

While efforts were focused on the growth possibilities of the twin, Boeing's product design teams were making their first exploratory forays into regional jet territory using the 737 as the basis for a future platform. At first the studies looked at a "737-250," which was smaller than a -200 with seating for around 100 and aimed at competition with the Fokker 100. Like the Netherlands-built aircraft, the study 737 was also proposed with the new Rolls-Royce Tay turbofan, although a CFM56-3 and P&W JT8D-400 were also options. However, all studies into the

The availability of the larger, new technology CFM56 engine reincarnated the 737. To enable the 60-inch-fan-diameter engine to fit on the wing, the bottom of the inlet lip was flattened. The engine was also moved forward, allowing it to be cantilevered off the leading edge. The rather odd-looking inlet shape is clearly visible in this view of a British Midland 737 scurrying in front of a Virgin Atlantic Airways 747.

The 737-300 fuselage was extended by 8 feet, 8 inches while the wingspan was increased 1 foot, 10 inches by adding an 11-inch extension to each wing tip. The wing leading-edge slat outboard of the nacelles, trailing-edge flaps, and flaptrack fairings were also improved, and extra lateral-control spoilers were added. The dorsal fin area was also increased, as can be seen emphasized in white paint on this brand-new Virgin Express 737-300 undergoing predelivery checks at Boeing Field. The extra spoilers are also clearly seen.

The cargo door of this 737-300QC (Quick Change) convertible freighter is just visible as this Lufthansa aircraft approaches to land. The fuselage is strengthened around the crown and sides to accept the 11-foot, 8-inch by 7-foot, 6-inch cargo door while the floor beams are also beefed up. This particular conversion was made by Colorado-based Pemco. Lufthansa was the launch customer for the 737 and maintained its association with the CFM56-powered versions until finally opting for Airbus in the 1990s.

smaller 737 abruptly halted in early 1986 when Boeing lost two competitions in quick succession to the British Aerospace 146 and the Fokker 100.

Within 12 months, however, the design team was back working on the small 737. This time, though, the target was different, and efforts were focused on a modern, quiet replacement for the original -200 series. The solution was elegantly simple: the newly termed 737-500 was now devised to carry 132 passengers in all-economy seating, making it almost 15-percent larger than the original proposition. Structurally it was virtually identical to the -300 and -400 but was shortened by 94 inches by the removal of a 54-inch plug aft and a 40-inch plug forward of the wing. The result was an overall length of 101 feet, 9 inches, just over 1 foot longer than the basic -200. The Series 500 was launched on May 20, 1987, with orders and options for 73 aircraft from Braathens SAFE, Euralair, and Maersk in Europe and Southwest in the United States. Within six months the order book had grown to 90, and development accelerated toward the first flight, which finally took place on June 30, 1989.

It was therefore fitting when, on February 15, 1991, a Series 500 aircraft became the 2,000th 737 to be delivered. The customer was Lufthansa, which, as original launch airline for the little Boeing jet, was also accepting its 100th 737. The aircraft was delivered via an ice-bound Frobisher Bay, where temperatures of -23 degrees Celsius froze the APU solid. As crew and passengers, the author among them, headed east over the North Atlantic during that dark February night, none could have guessed that yet another spectacular chapter in the 737 story was about to unfold.

Colorado-based Western Pacific was among a new generation of airlines that used flamboyant liveries and even advertising to raise their profile. Despite these efforts and the use of highly economical 737-300s, the airline folded in 1998.

The 737-400 became the longest version produced when it was first rolled out in 1988. The fuselage was stretched by 10 feet over the -300, making it 119 feet, 7 inches long overall. The additional length can be gauged in this view of a British Airways -400 as it nears Heathrow.

Production
soared with the CFM56-powered
versions, and in January 1998 Boeing
delivered the 3,000th "Classic"
aircraft, a 737-400 for Alaska Airlines.
Only four months later the
introduction of the Next Generation
pushed sales through the 4,000 mark.

Another early 747-121 in the colors of launch customer Pan American brings Gulf War troops back home to the United States in April 1991. *Clipper Ocean Herald* began life with the airline as *Clipper Red Jacket* when delivered in January 1970 but changed to its new name in 1980. The aircraft was withdrawn from use little more than a year after this shot was taken at New York's JFK International.

6
Queen of the Skies

Boeing's bold 1952 decision to go ahead with the self-funded Dash 80 passed into company mythology as the $16 million gamble of the decade. Yet only 14 years later Boeing outdid even this feat by risking the very company itself on a mammoth new $1 billion project that was to revolutionize global air travel and make Boeing into a household name around the world. The new airliner was set to become one of the most significant aircraft ever created and was called the 747.

Astonishingly, the 747 was intended to be little more than a stopgap. Big aircraft companies in the 1960s were gearing up for the battle of the supersonic transports, which were confidently expected to rule the skies from the 1970s onwards. Yet, as history was to prove, the big jet was to carve itself a giant slice of the market all by itself, eclipsing the competition and establishing Boeing as the dominant jetliner manufacturer for the rest of the century.

Although Boeing's gamble with the 747 almost failed in the crisis years of the early 1970s, the aircraft survived and went on to become highly profitable, helping bring in more than $130 billion dollars over the next three decades. By 1998, the world fleet of more than 1,100 active aircraft had carried over 2.2 billion people, or roughly 40 percent of the world's population. This unprecedented flow of travelers had an inevitable effect on global society, speedily spreading ideas and promoting cultural interchange on a scale unimaginable in the past. The 747 was the first, and largest, of the new widebody jets that led this travel explosion. The aircraft is therefore unique in history as a peaceful force that altered the face of world society—an impact that none could have foreseen in 1962 when the story really began.

The 747 came about, as with many significant engineering feats, through an almost bizarre set of events and circumstances. Most historians agree that if these events had not come together during a seven or eight year window in the 1960s, the 747 may never have been born at all—and certainly not on the vast scale that we know today. The period begins with the Cuban missile crisis of 1962 when the Cold War between NATO and the Soviet-led Warsaw Pact countries threatened to erupt into all-out nuclear war. It ends at the beginning of the 1970s when Boeing was deep in debt, the 747 program in trouble, and the world's economy was faltering after a decade of boom.

In 1962 the USAF, concerned about its lack of strategic airlift capacity highlighted by growing Cold War tensions, set up Project Forecast to gather data for new aircraft projects. One that emerged from the study was formally defined in the CX-HLS (cargo experimental-heavy logistics system) competition, which pitted Boeing, Douglas, and Lockheed in head-to-head competition. All three proposed gigantic aircraft that looked similar to one another with high wings and cavernous fuselages.

A much simpler variable-pivot flap design was adopted as a weight-saving measure for the 747SP. Seen here in this evening takeoff view, the flap helped reduce almost 12,500 pounds off the weight of the wing.

With
the names of its first flight crew still painted by the cockpit windows, the first 747-100, *City of Everett*, pushes its nose over the fence as if in search of another job. The 747 was brought out of retirement to act as an engine testbed for the 777 program. The large weights attached to the nose leg help balance the aircraft, which is pictured at Boeing Field without any engines.

Boeing believed it was in the winning seat with its design and long history of supplying the USAF with most of its biggest bombers and transports, yet it was in for a shock when Lockheed's C-5A Galaxy was announced as the victor.

There is a persistent myth that Boeing simply rubbed away the camouflage from its CX-HLS contender, painted it white, and rechristened it the 747. Apart from sheer scale, the only real link between the two projects in reality was the huge, new technology, high-bypass-ratio engines that had been developed to compete for the airlifter. The leap in aircraft scale required a similar leap in engine power, which had to be virtually doubled to around 40,000 pounds of thrust for the CX-HLS requirement. The two large U.S. engine makers, GE and P&W, had both come up with new powerplants derived from a common ancestor, the USAF's Lightweight Gas Generator

(LWGG) technology demonstrator program of the 1950s. The GE engine became the TF39, which became the world's first production high-bypass turbofan. The LWGG also spawned P&W's STF200 and JTF14 demonstrator engines that led to the JT9D. These vastly more powerful engines were therefore available to Boeing at just the right time. Without these developments, the 747 could never have been conceived.

Another factor was the surging U.S. and world economy. Air travel was growing at the unbelievable rate of 15 percent a year, thanks in part to the new generation of safe, reliable jetliners like the 707 and DC-8. The airlines began asking the manufacturers to study bigger aircraft to meet the demand and, to its dismay, Boeing found itself unable to compete on equal terms with Douglas. The California-based aircraft maker was developing the DC-8 "Super Sixties" series that could seat up to 269 and fly ranges of up to 4,500 nautical miles. The DC-8 was much easier to stretch than the 707 because it had tall (63-inch) main gear legs and a more modest sweep angle of 30.6 degrees, which reduced the takeoff and rotation angle. Boeing could have stretched the 707 and spent time studying versions (such as the proposed 707-820/506) more than 56 feet longer than the -320 with seats for up to 279. In the end it decided that the huge changes needed to the wing, undercarriage, and fuselage were just not worth spending the money on.

The design process leading to the 747 began immediately after Lockheed won the CX-HLS contract. Joe Sutter, who subsequently was known as the "Father of the 747," was recalled from leave and put in charge of the design project in August 1965 as chief project engineer. "I got about 100 engineers, and we began making drawings of the kinds of airplanes we could make using these high-bypass-ratio engines. We did not know what size to make the airplane, so we cartooned, if you will, three different sizes—a 250-seater, a 300-seater, and a 350-seater. Then we took the brochures to most of the major airlines like Pan Am, BOAC, Japan Air Lines (JAL), Lufthansa, and so on, and asked them the question: What size do you want? Pan Am, very definitely, wanted the larger size, and practically everybody else voted for the larger size. To be honest, it was a sort of shock because the 707 carried 120 people, and suddenly they wanted an airplane two and a half times the size of that."

CREATING A JUMBO

Pan Am, and particularly its chairman, Juan Trippe, became the driving force behind the new project during the winter of 1965 as the design began to come together. More than 200 initial concepts were considered, and these were gradually narrowed to a smaller group of 50 promising designs. At this stage some were still high-wing designs sharing high commonality with the CX-HLS concepts, some were "mid-wing," and nearly all were double-deckers. "Everybody was intrigued with double-deckers," said Sutter, who was not impressed. "The group working for me decided that was the wrong way to go. If you had about 1,000 passengers, then a double-decker works, but if you're designing for 500 to 600 passengers, you end up with a big wing on a short, stubby airplane." Every operational aspect of such a design was a problem, Sutter believed. He called the short, fat double-decker a "clumsy airplane."

While the team wrestled with the fuselage cross-section, other parts fell into place. "We knew we wanted to have a swept-wing and just put the engines on that. So the basic architecture was well defined," said Sutter. It was at this stage that the supersonic transport (SST) began to have the most dramatic impact on the final outcome of the shape. The Boeing SST project was well under way at the time of the 747's conception and was already roughly defined as a 250–350 seat, Mach 2.7 aircraft. Boeing's entry, the 2707, was competing against Lockheed for the American SST program, and optimism was high over its success. "Many of the airlines, and the people here at Boeing, thought that the 747 was an airplane with a limited future because the SST was going to take all the business," recalled Sutter. Forecasts at the time predicted a market for up to 1,250 SSTs between 1972 and 1978. The only other serious contender, the Anglo-French Concorde, was expected to take "at least 250" of this. No one could have guessed that the U.S. Congress would terminate the American SST in March 1971 or that Concorde production would stop after only 14 production standard aircraft were made.

To Sutter's team in 1965, it seemed inevitable that the 747 would be relegated to cargo duty within a decade or so. They, therefore, made the extraordinary decision to design it from scratch as a freighter. To make it into a viable freighter, the team worked out designs to accommodate two seagoing 8x8-foot containers and essentially

Lying forgotten in a Florida backwater by Kennedy Space Center, this pile of scrap metal has more to do with the shape of the 747 than any other factor. This is the remains of a full-scale mockup of the Boeing 2707-200 Supersonic Transport (SST), which everyone, including the 747 design team, was convinced would soon rule the sky. This led directly to Boeing's "widebody" concept, which allowed the 747 to be quickly transformed into a freighter for the time when, it was believed, the SST would take over the main passenger routes. History would prove otherwise.

The historic but sadly shabby-looking former Pan Am aircraft *Clipper Juan Trippe* stands derelict at San Bernardino International in late 1997. This was the second 747 built and was originally called *Jet Clipper America* with the registration N747PA. It was also one of the first to be involved in a serious accident when it hit the runway lights on takeoff from San Francisco in July 1971. The impact ripped the belly open and disabled three of the four hydraulic systems, but the crew was able to bring it back for landing, proving the benefit of the elaborate built-in redundancy.

drew large circles around the main deck freight pallets until they had a cross-section. The big single deck was also able to seat up to 10 across, with two or more aisles running along its length. "Right near the contract signing we conceived this wide single deck. Of all the decisions we made, the most important was selecting the wide single deck. It gave us an airplane that was efficient and extremely flexible and was one of the main reasons for its success," said Sutter. Seemingly at a stroke, Sutter's team had created the world's first widebody jetliner.

The decision to design the aircraft with a main deck cargo capability also drove the development of the hinged nose to allow straight-through freight loading. This meant the flight deck had to be located somewhere other than its normal position in the nose. A lower flight deck was briefly considered and was nicknamed the "anteater" as a result of its droop snout. In the end a high flight deck design was adopted, which placed the cockpit above the main deck in a small upper deck section. The flight deck had to be faired into the forward upper fuselage, creating the now familiar "hump" of the 747. Strictly speaking, the 747 emerged as a double-decker but not on the scale of the initial concepts. In later life the upper deck played a more prominent role in the aircraft but not in 1965.

Under increasing pressure from Pan Am, the Boeing board finally authorized the monstrous aircraft project in March 1966. Malcolm Stamper, the original 747 program vice president and general manager, recalled in a *Flight International* interview: "I remember everyone looking at Bill Allen down the table, and it was his call, whether to bet the company on it. The size of the airplane itself was not that much of a technical breakthrough—it was the fundamental scale of the project. I think it was the greatest industrial undertaking in the history of the company."

The following month Pan Am launched the program by converting the letter of intent for 25, originally placed in December 1965, into a conditional order at the then staggering price of $20 million apiece. Boeing began clearing a huge site north of Seattle adjacent to Paine Field in Everett where the 747 final assembly would take place. The site had already been earmarked for manufacture of the CX-HLS aircraft but was now devoted to the new 747. The costs quickly began to mount as the detailed design accelerated, and the construction of the Everett site had begun by the time full-scale production was authorized in July 1966.

UNVEILING A GIANT

When the first 747 rolled out of the Everett factory doors at 11:10 **A.M.** on September 30, 1968, most observers were awed by the vast size of the aircraft. At 231 feet, 4 inches in length, it was around 80 feet longer than the

Boeing's first large-scale market success with the 747 came with the -200 Series, of which 389 were built in all versions. The growth of the -200 also gave General Electric and Rolls-Royce a chance to get aboard. Here a Rolls-Royce RB.211-powered Air Pacific lifts off for Fiji on a humid afternoon at Los Angeles International. The 747 was the first jetliner to be available with engines from all three major manufacturers.

707-320 and towered to a height of 63 feet, 5 inches, or roughly a third again as high.

Its complex genetic heritage included something from every previous generation of Boeing jet-powered aircraft. From the B-47 it took the concept of podded engines, spoilers, and sharply swept-wing and tail surfaces. From the B-52 it inherited the all-moving horizontal tail and aerodynamic breakthrough of the thick wing root. The 707 provided much of the configuration blueprint, systems know-how, and further refinements of lessons learned on the earlier bombers. From the 727 it took larger versions of its extraordinary triple-slotted flaps and other high-lift innovations. It also inherited the multiple redundant hydraulic flight-control-systems concept developed for the trijet and further honed for the 737. From the baby twinjet it also took advantage of much of the newer materials technology that was vital for saving weight.

The scale of the 747 demanded that each of these inherited features, plus a wide variety of new ones, be developed to new levels of safety and performance. In fact, the word "safety" was at the forefront of the design team's mind from the very beginning. "The thing about the 747 design that's different from other airplanes is the sheer amount of redundancy," said Sutter. "Here we were

designing a 350-passenger airplane, which was huge at the time, and safety was the biggest single issue."

The result was split control surfaces, inboard and outboard ailerons, split spoilers, elevators, and rudders. All were powered by four hydraulic systems, double the redundancy of previous designs, and were backed up with manual reversion capability. The in-built redundancy was nowhere more apparent than the undercarriage, which consisted of four main legs and one nose leg supporting a total of 18 wheels. The enormous gear not only provided added safety but helped cushion the weight of the monster on landing and spread the "footprint" of the 747 to that of the 707 during takeoff and taxiing.

The safety benefits of the multiply redundant gear and hydraulic systems proved themselves within only months of the 747's first entering service when Pan Am's flagship aircraft, N747PA, hit the approach light gantry on takeoff at San Francisco International in July 1971. The crew misjudged the takeoff speed and distance and abruptly hauled the 747 into the air at the end of the runway only to scrape its belly through the lights. The tremendous impact thrust the right body landing gear up into the cargo compartment, tore two wheels from the other body gear, and disabled *three* of the four hydraulic systems. The severely crippled aircraft staggered into the air with parts of

▲ Cathay
Pacific 747-200, specially painted to celebrate the 1997 hand-over of Hong Kong from the British to the Chinese, makes its final approach to the former territory's Kai Tak International Airport. The Asian economic crisis struck shortly after the transition, and the resulting collapse in passenger loads forced Cathay to sell off many of its trusty -200s.

the gantry and other objects sticking through the cabin floor and up into the tail section. Despite the heavy damage, the crew fought for control and managed to bring the 747 in for a safe landing. The aircraft was later repaired and returned to service.

The hydraulics provided actuation for all primary flight controls; all secondary controls (except leading-edge flaps); and landing gear retraction, extension, gear steering, and wheel braking. Systems 1 and 4 could be used for all purposes, while Systems 2 and 3 were normally used for flight control only. Each system was pressurized to 3,000 psi by a pump mounted on the engine, backed up by pneumatic pumps. System 4 also had a third, electrical power source. Each primary flight control axis received power from all four hydraulic systems. With the exception of the spoilers, each control surface was powered by a dual tandem hydraulic actuator supplied by two of the four main systems.

The design aim of so much redundancy was to ensure survivability in a wide variety of potential disaster scenarios. This included retaining control if an entire engine dropped off the wing or even if an entire outer wing section detached or was torn away. Other scenarios included the loss of an upper-fin section or an outboard section of tailplane or elevator. Flight control could even be maintained in a glide with all engines failed or two hydraulic systems out. As it had already proved by 1971, it also allowed landings to be made with only one system remaining.

Much of the emphasis on safety was concentrated on the wing design, which incorporated a rare third spar as far outboard as the number 1 and number 4 engine struts. The wing shape and size was optimized for the design range, aircraft weight, fuel capacity, and efficiency. "The span was first determined by the aerodynamic requirements of getting the takeoff weight into the air, getting to

Virgin
Atlantic Airways' "Scarlet Lady" blushes in the glow of evening sunshine as it leaves London Heathrow on a September evening in 1997. Variable-camber leading-edge flaps are clearly visible on the outboard leading edge, as are the inboard Krueger flaps. The sunlight also picks out the triple-slotted trailing-edge flaps and the outline of the complex main undercarriage bay doors, which closed just seconds before this image was captured.

A hard-working Varig 747-300 touches down at Los Angeles International. The Brazilian carrier operated -300s on a constant rotation between Rio de Janeiro, Sao Paulo, Los Angeles, and Tokyo. The -300 was not the big seller that Boeing had hoped for, but it pioneered the stretched upper deck, which became the basis for the very popular -400 Series.

Brakes,
reverse thrust, full flaps, and spoilers slow a Corsair 747SP as it rolls out on landing at Los Angeles. Boeing traded airframe weight for fuel to give the SP long-range capability. Typical range with 305 passengers and 20,000 pounds of cargo is around 6,600 nautical miles, making the handful of survivors a popular low-cost option for some operators.

a good initial cruise altitude, and ending up with a reasonable approach speed so pilots would have an easy time landing the aircraft," said Sutter. The 747 was also designed for long-range, so Boeing upped the cruise speed capability to Mach 0.85. The key ingredient for this was the sweep angle, which was eventually set at 37 degrees and 30 minutes, sharper than the 35 degrees of the B-47, B-52, and 707, and five degrees greater than the 727.

Most of the late design refinements to the wing, including the positioning of the engines and the arrangement of the flaps, were caused by discoveries made during elaborate wind-tunnel tests. In all, some 14,000 hours of wind-tunnel tests were performed on the 747, compared with around 6,000 hours on the 727, the next most time-intensive Boeing jetliner design at that time. To ensure that its results were accurate, Boeing built two exact-scale 9-foot models with working flight control surfaces and other

detailed features. The two models, each costing the equivalent of a real Douglas DC-6 in the mid-1960s, led to the adoption of many changes that fully justified the test effort's multi-million dollar cost. These included the triple-slotted flap system, a new system of rudder and elevator control, a revised tail design, and a more smoothly tapered tail cone.

The final wing design was highly tapered in cross-section with a sharp leading edge and nearly 4-percent "washout" to the outboard section. This was introduced after wind-tunnel work, elasticity tests on a structural model of the wing, and analysis of spanwise loadings. The wing tips themselves were "sawn-off," or straight edged, which made them slightly less aerodynamic but a lot easier to make. It also restricted the already-large aircraft's wingspan to 195 feet, 8 inches, thus keeping it manageable at airports around the world.

A major feature heavily influenced by the wind tunnel was the positioning of the engines. Originally they were

designed to be closer inboard at 30 percent and 50 percent, where they would present fewer asymmetry problems in case of failure. The struts holding the engines were hung under the wing, rather than on and slightly over the leading edge as on the 707, to conform with flow conditions at high-speed cruise and to reduce their effect on the flaps. These were originally designed to be double-slotted and were to create extra lift by taking advantage of induced flow from the engines. However, this arrangement showed that too many trim changes would be needed with different power settings, so it was dropped. Instead, a version of the recently developed 727 triple-slotted flap was used, and the engines were located at 40 percent and 71 percent, where their exhaust came between, rather than through, the flap sections.

A benefit of this revised flap design was the creation of a gap in the trailing edge. Boeing hoped to make do with a single, outboard aileron, but recalling lessons from

as far back as the B-47, inserted the inboard aileron into the new gap. The decision was sound, as flight tests proved the roll-control authority of the outer aileron alone to be insufficient. The relatively narrow leading edge of the "peaky" aerofoil section also demanded a few innovations from the design team. As a result, the variable-camber leading-edge flaps were made from a flexible fiberglass material that folded flat under the wing when not in use and yet could be extended into a smooth contour for low-speed flight. Each wing packed 10 variable-camber flaps and 3 Krueger flaps on the leading edge.

Late changes were also made to the shape and structure of the fuselage. The enormous scale of the 747 posed new challenges in the design of the body. Unlike the B-52, which was the largest jet aircraft flying at the time, virtually the whole fuselage volume of the 747 had to be pressurized rather than simply the crew sections. The B-52

The SP is 47 feet, 1 inch shorter than the standard 747, resulting in a 50-percent reduction in pitch inertia and a 9-percent forward shift of gravity. Despite these changes, Boeing adapted the flying controls to make it handle exactly like its larger sibling. The taller tail fin and shorter body is emphasized in this side view of a Mandarin Airlines SP approaching Hong Kong.

131

A United
747-400 touches down. Like the previous generations before it, the large wing area, huge flaps, and multiple undercarriage combined to provide a cushioning effect, which helped make most landings trouble-free. Note the spoilers deploying as touchdown occurs. The crew begins to flare the 747 gently at around 50 feet and begins closing the throttles at 30 feet while holding the stick back slightly against any nose-down pitch motion. By 10 feet, with power at idle, the 747 mushes into a ground-effect cushion of its own creation.

body was built around heavy longerons, or large fore-and-aft structural members, whereas the pressurized 747 required a widebody made from a combination of stringers, skin, and frame. The body design was also affected by wind-tunnel tests that showed that the original blisterlike fairing for the flight deck generated way too much drag. The familiar, fully integrated flight deck design was introduced instead, leading to the development of the larger upper deck. The use of "area ruling" design principles (only recently developed for fighter designs) led to the unusual slab-sided look of the flight deck area.

The flight deck itself contained some major firsts for any Boeing. In addition to the normal VOR/DME (distance measuring equipment), ADF (automatic direction finding), and Loran (long-range navigation) receivers, the 747 was the first commercial aircraft to have an inertial navigation system (INS) designed from the outset as standard equipment. The INS had been developed for U.S. nuclear submarines and enhanced for the Apollo space program. It allowed for accurate point-to-point navigation without the need for ground-based aids, and each aircraft was fitted with three units to provide a primary reference for both navigation and attitude control.

Another advance was the automatic flight-control system, which integrated the dual autopilot, flight director, dual channel yaw damper, and autothrottle. The combination was achieved because much of the computer capability required for the autopilot was identical to that needed for the flight director. The autopilot provided fully automatic and heading control via flight computers or optional control-wheel steering. Three identical Sperry (later part of Honeywell) autopilot/flight director computers formed the core of the system. They provided the fail-operational safety margin needed to ensure Category II approach and automatic landings even if a computer failed.

More redundancy was built into the yaw damper, or

stability augmentation system, which was designed to damp any natural side-to-side (yaw) oscillations. The system was duplicated so that one channel drove the top rudder section and the other drove the lower section, and it provided extra safety if one part of the rudder was damaged or if one system gave a faulty output. Each of the channels for the yaw damper system had four sensors providing data to a separate computer, and yaw itself was sensed by a rate gyro.

Another significant change from previous Boeing aircraft, of all sizes and types, was the large amount of advanced lightweight honeycomb, fiberglass, and other new material used in the 747. "There was a time when the whole project went into a tailspin," said Sutter, who recalled the crisis in early 1967 when it became apparent that the huge aircraft was gaining too much weight. A "Lift and Thrift" program was urgently brought into play to cut down the weight, and a task force was assembled to study other slimming initiatives. Largely as a result of this, a polyvinyl chloride (PVC-filled fiberglass sandwich sprayed with a bonded coating of aluminum) was used for the big 80-foot fairings where the wing joined the body, as well as other areas. The use of the material, commonly called Nomex, represented the biggest use of plastics applied to an aircraft at that time.

FLIGHT TESTING AND CHANGES

The ambitious design, development, and manufacturing schedule was matched by the flight test program, which began eight weeks behind schedule, on February 9, 1969. Flying qualities were better than expected, and the aircraft "almost lands itself," reported project pilot Jack Waddell at the conclusion of the first sortie. The initial test phase was marked by problems with engines and, to a lesser extent, flutter.

The engine difficulties were partly related to the incredibly fast pace of the entire genesis of the program and the fact that P&W's task of developing a reliable high-bypass-ratio turbofan for rigorous airline use was as hard, if not harder, than that of Boeing's airframe responsibility. The late increase in the weight of the 747 also posed problems for P&W, which had been aiming its initial 41,000-pound-thrust JT9D at the planned takeoff weight of 690,000 pounds. Even before first flight, however, the 747 had already grown to 710,000 pounds, which required an immediate jump in power from the engines to 42,000 pounds for the bulk of the test effort. The engine maker

Asian-based airlines dominated the 747-400 order book with more than half the fleet operated in the region by the mid-1990s. The economic problems of 1998 caused the first check on expansion, affecting deliveries of new aircraft to carriers like Thai and Asiana. The Saudi Arabian -400 at the bottom of this picture was one of five ordered as part of a massive $7.5-billion deal negotiated in late 1995.

The unmatched high capacity and long-range of the 747 made it an ideal flagship for airlines with far-flung destinations like South African Airways 747-312 ZS-SAJ, which is seen operating this brightly liveried aircraft from London Heathrow to Johannesburg and Cape Town.

was forced to quickly grow the engine even further to 43,500 pounds thrust and then 45,000 pounds, leapfrogging the traditional growth pathway.

Compared to the 707's JT3D engine with a fan bypass ratio of 1.4:1 and a compressor ratio of 13:1, the JT9D produced a massive fan bypass ratio of 5:1 and almost twice the compression ratio. This, coupled with an increase in turbine inlet temperatures and approximately 40-percent increase in core engine flow, pumped out more than double the thrust of the JT3D. The big volume of air passing through the fan also shrouded noise, made the engine more environmentally friendly, and reduced thrust-specific fuel consumption by 40 percent. But the fast pace, combined with the bold technological initiatives in the design, gave Boeing and P&W considerable headaches in the early years.

The improved compressor achieved a compression ratio of 24 in just 15 stages, compared with 13 in 16 stages on the JT3D. A key technology behind this seemingly magic achievement was the use of variable stators in three stages of the high-pressure compressor—the first such application in a U.S. commercial jet engine. These helped maintain adequate margin for starting, acceleration, and part-power operation and were controlled by arms and linkages arranged in rings around the casing. The problems began when these linkages began sticking in one position, and they were only solved by liberal use of lubricating oil.

The engine also suffered from overheating caused by an insensitive barometric fuel-control system. In most conditions it worked well, but in a crosswind at ground idle (58-percent high- pressure spool rpm), it could not keep pace with variations in airflow and pressure. The system normally judged how much fuel to feed the combustors according to Pitot pressure at the face of the engine intake. If these signs were misread, the fuel-air ratio became too rich, which, in turn, led to turbine overheating. The engine was also difficult to start unless the aircraft was pointed into wind. Reverse flow through the compressor produced similar overheating and "hung-start" problems to the crosswind scenario.

The biggest engine problem of all was distortion, or "ovalization," of the compressor, turbine, and exhaust casing. This turned out to be more of a problem with the way the engine was mounted on the wing rather than the engine itself, but it baffled engineers for several tense months during the early testing and service entry phase. Although not dangerous in itself, the ovalization phenomenon caused the compressor and turbine blades to rub against the casing. As the efficiency of a jet engine hinges on maintaining the highest possible pressure through these sections of the powerplant, any gaps that appear through the rubbing down of the blade tips and lining can quickly eat into the fuel efficiency and thrust margins. The engine loses power and efficiency and runs hotter to achieve the same thrust as before, thus wearing out parts more quickly and reducing reliability.

The problem was made even more urgent because P&W was behind the "thrust curve" as it was, and it needed every ounce of available power. The engine maker did everything it could to try to fix the problem. It did all sorts of tests to work out why the turbine case was only rubbing at the base of the engine and what it could do about it. P&W tried special pin seals in the low-pressure turbine, pre-ovalized abradable seals and even an offset high-pressure compressor casing. But the problems just got worse. By July 1969, up to 0.043 inch of bending had been measured at the combustor chamber case and 0.050 inch at the turbine. The company began stiffening the outside of the engine, too, and managed to cut "ovality" by 12 percent at the exhaust and 15 percent at the turbine.

With completed airframes pouring off the Everett line with no engines hanging off them, the pressure from Boeing and the airlines on P&W was immense. In near desperation P&W began looking at the way the engine was

connected to the wing and quickly realized it was onto something. The engine was so big, heavy (8,600 pounds apiece), and long that it bowed, or flexed, as the 747 rotated for takeoff. The engine was attached to the strut, or pylon, via a single-point front pickup on top of the fan case. P&W had opted for this method instead of the usual side lugs aft of the fan on the main carcass because it helped keep the cowling thin and aerodynamic. Now it designed two 45-degree thrust transfer members that were attached to two other points on the exhaust casing.

The result was an immediate reduction in bending of 30 percent and a cut in ovality of 10 percent. P&W knew it was on the right track. More could be done, however, so it developed a 45-degree "Y"-shaped frame, which transferred thrust loads to the intermediate compressor casing. The final fix was a similar, inverted 60-degree "Y-frame," which cut out all ovalization where it counted most at the turbine casing and reduced bending movement by 80 percent. P&W, Boeing, and the airlines breathed a collective sigh of relief, and the JT9D began a happier phase in its life. More powerful versions of the JT9D producing up to 56,000 pounds thrust were eventually developed before P&W switched to the very successful PW4000 derivative family.

Flutter was much less of an issue than engines for the 747 test effort but still posed some challenges. Flutter was a feared phenomenon that produced a self-sustaining and sometimes destructive vibration of the airframe. Boeing expected some flutter but hoped the positioning of the engines on struts well forward of the flexural axis of the wing would help counteract the tendency. Some instability was eventually found at the highest cruise-speed levels at around Mach 0.86. The solutions eventually selected included an adjustment to the fuel feed system that changed the weight distribution in the outboard wing section, which was most susceptible to the condition. Another was the use of depleted uranium weights in the number one and four engine struts. These "shot bags" added around 700 pounds per outboard engine in the test aircraft. In production aircraft the area was stiffened rather than weighted down.

"CLASSIC" DERIVATIVES

Static tests of the base-line aircraft proved beyond doubt that further growth to higher gross weights was possible without the need for fundamental and expensive modifications. As a result, the 747 began a series of steady growth steps which continued for the remainder of the century. By early 1998 airlines were offered a new Increased Gross Weight (IGW) version of the 747-400 that had a maximum takeoff weight capability of 910,000 pounds—around 200,000 pounds more than the first 747-100, a difference roughly equal to the maximum weight of the Dash 80.

The first major variant developed from the basic -100 Series was the -200B. It was structurally

The gear begins to swing as this Cathay Pacific -400 begins its long flight from England to Hong Kong. The winglets and extended span of 211 feet, 5 inches are evident in this view. Most of the increase is made up by 6-foot-span extensions on each tip. The winglet produced a 3-percent increase in range on long-distance flights.

The crew, just visible in this nose-on view, is 29 feet above the ground on touchdown. Crew members are advised to aim for a spot on the runway roughly 1,600 to 2,000 feet from the threshold to avoid undershooting.

strengthened with thicker skins and stronger wing stringers, spars, landing-gear beams, flaps, and a beefed-up rib-and-wing panel splice. The fuselage had stronger gear supports, keel beam, Section 44 bulkheads, skins, stringers, and some door frames. Major components of the landing gear were also individually strengthened and were fitted with 49x17-inch, 30-ply main and nose tires. The empennage was also strengthened with revisions to the horizontal stabilizer torque box and center section. The trailing-edge flap actuation system and leading-edge flaps were also beefed up. Maximum takeoff weight was also increased to 775,000 pounds and fuel load increased to 51,430 U.S. gallons.

The -200 Series became popular and quickly out-stripped the sales of the -100, particularly when General Electric engines and later Rolls-Royce engines became available as optional powerplants. Together with freighter and combi versions, the -200 Series became the most popular version of the 747 until the advent of the -400. Sales began to wind down in the mid-1980s as the -300 was introduced and Boeing notched up the final few sales, ending the run with the delivery of the 393rd aircraft (a -281F [SCD] to Nippon Cargo Airlines) in 1989.

Even though the -200 continued to sell well throughout the late 1970s, Boeing continued to study new derivatives of the aircraft to meet airline demands for more capacity and range. In June 1980, after months of study, it gave the go-ahead to a modest stretch of the upper deck. The new version was eventually called the 747-300 but began life either as the stretched upper deck (SUD), or extended upper deck (EUD). The hump was extended aft by 23 feet, 4 inches, allowing the SUD/EUD to seat about 44 more than the standard -200B. In effect, this created room for up to 91 passengers on the top deck in an all-economy configuration or a theoretical maximum capacity for 110. The deck was reached with a new straight stairway that led up and aft from the main deck, replacing the original spiral stairway.

The -300 was both good news and bad for Boeing's customers. The good news was that capacity was increased to a theoretical maximum of 660, though no airline ever carried more than 580 on a regular basis. The extended upper hump also offered unexpected aerodynamic benefits, allowing the typical maximum cruise speed to rise from Mach 0.84 to 0.85. The bad news was that the extra weight of the top deck structure added around 10,000 pounds to the overall weight and limited range to 5,600 nautical miles with 452 passengers. The result was a bit disappointing to most airlines, as the benefits were not all that great. The payload was an improvement, but the airlines still wanted more range. As a result the -300 did not prosper as Boeing had hoped, and only 81 were delivered, of which 21 were combis. The last delivery came in September 1990. The SUD/EUD concept was sound, however, and a further 14 747-100B and -200s were modified with the extended upper deck. As with so many other Boeings before it, however, the changes developed for the -300 provided the vital next step to yet another generation. In this case, the structural extension to the upper deck was the basis for the most important 747 derivative produced so far—the Series -400.

Before looking at the -400, however, it is important not to neglect one other significant variant, the 747SP. Although by Boeing standards the SP was not a commercial success, with only 45 delivered, the development of this short-bodied version taught the company valuable lessons for the future and pioneered important new concepts such as the common flight deck.

The 747SP, or "SB" for short body, as it was originally called, was Boeing's answer to the emerging threat of long-range trijets such as the extended range Lockheed L-1011 and McDonnell Douglas DC-10-30/40. Although Boeing was well into studies of an all-new 7X7 design that would one day fit the bill (eventually to emerge as the 767), the company was under pressure from airlines for a quicker solution. After thorough trade studies Boeing made the decision to shorten the 747 rather than develop an all-new product. The concept was simple. "Some of the sales and management people laughed at us, but we thought we could make it work by taking the weight out of it and giving it the right passenger/range combination," said Joe Sutter, who helped originate the project.

Unlike half-baked studies dating from 1968 when Boeing toyed with a trijet version of the 747 to compete on transcontinental routes with the DC-10 and L-1011, the SP was to retain the same four-jet configuration of the base-line aircraft. Trijet arrangements were studied, however, and included some bizarre configurations with two engines under one wing and one under the other. It also studied more conventional trijet arrangements with the tail engine buried at the root of the fin, which, in some studies, supported a T-tail derived largely from the 727. Although the trijet saved money in terms of weight, cost, and fuel burn (a major concern in the midst of the Arab oil embargo at the time), the complications of adapting the 747 to such a new arrangement far outweighed the benefits.

Like the 747 and 707 before it, the launch of the 747SP depended on Pan Am. The U.S. carrier had a firm requirement for an aircraft for its "long-thin" routes and was close to signing a deal with McDonnell Douglas for the DC-10 when Boeing pitched the SP. The promise of commonality with the standard 747 and superior performance won over Pan Am, which formally announced an order for 10 SPs in September 1973.

The aircraft was sized to carry 281 in a typical mixed-class layout, more than 100 fewer than the equivalent -200B. The fuselage was cut back by 48 feet, 4 inches, making it 176 feet, 9 inches long, or almost exactly the same length as the 767-300 that would follow a decade later. The unusual contours of the 747 prevented Boeing from simply cutting out fuselage plugs to make the SP. Instead a section of fuselage forward of the front wing spar was removed, as was the upper section immediately aft. This latter part was removed to make room for the fairing over the raised upper deck, which now became flush with the fuselage at mid-chord rather than by the leading edge. The large wing-body fairing was replaced with a smaller "cropped" fillet, and extra soundproofing was added to the upper lobe. The center section was redesigned to save weight, and a new aft fuselage section was produced to replace sections removed from forward of the pressure bulkhead.

The SP tail height was increased to compensate for the reduced fin moment arm. The base of the fin was 38 inches lower than the standard aircraft, and an extra 60 inches was added to the top. The result was a tail 24 inches taller overall than the 747, producing a visibly slender tail unit. The rudder was also double-hinged to boost control authority while the tips of the horizontal stabilizers were extended by 60 inches for the same reason. A revised dorsal fin was added to the base of the fin, where the unusually steep contouring created a pronounced dip in the roof of the fuselage.

The main changes to the wing concerned a switch to a much simpler single-slotted flap system, replacing the complex triple-slotted arrangement of the larger aircraft. The lower overall weight of the SP and resulting reduced wing loading of 120 pounds per square foot compared to 140 pounds per square foot for the -200B also meant that the structure of the wing itself could be significantly lighter. It was therefore built with reduced gauge spars, skins, ribs, and stringers in the wing box and center section. Together with the simpler flaps, the revised structure was 12,500 pounds lighter than the 88,537-pound wing set of the 747-100. The fuselage was also lighter by more than 11,000 pounds, while the enlarged tail was actually 1,500 pounds heavier. The overall result was a saving of 44,100 pounds over the -100, with an operating empty weight of 315,000 pounds.

In service the 747SP proved to be an exceptionally able performer, breaking many altitude, range, and speed records, some of which were still unbroken 20 years later. Despite its technical success, the SP was aimed at a market niche that had virtually disappeared by the time the first aircraft were being delivered. The rise of most cost-effective trijet competition and even the success of Boeing's own -200B family proved too much for the SP, which withered on the vine despite strenuous marketing. The last few sales trickled out in the 1980s, and the last aircraft was delivered in 1987 to the United Arab Emirates.

747-400

The importance of the development of the -400 Series to the 747 story and to Boeing in general cannot be overstated. The 1985 launch of the new version completely revitalized sales of the 747, which virtually doubled as a result. It also ensured Boeing's dominance of the megajet arena for the remainder of the century and provided the sound financial and marketing footing for its next major widebody venture, the 777.

The -400 is also a classic example of how new technology can lead to the virtual resurrection of even a "classic" product. The process had begun with the 1979 decision to go ahead with the all-new 757 and 767. These twin developments injected a vast amount of new design, materials, avionics and systems technology, and know-how into the company. It also stimulated airline awareness of these advances, which were then plowed into the rebirth of the 737 beginning with the -300 Series. This was the process that caught up with the 747, which was, by then, facing the rising tide of technology on all fronts. Airbus Industrie, an active proponent of high technology in civil aerospace, was studying a pair of long-range fly-by-wire airliners. McDonnell Douglas was developing a radical upgrade for the DC-10, which effectively developed into an all-new trijet called the MD-11.

The "advanced Series 300" was Boeing's initial response. It looked virtually identical to the -300 apart from prominent winglets, and all the significant changes were beneath the skin. These were aimed at meeting five major design objectives. First, it would feature a raft of upgraded technology. Second, the interior would be given a new look. Third, range would be increased by 1,000 nautical miles in response to airline demand. Fourth, fuel burn would be reduced by as much as 37 percent compared to the early -100s. Lastly, the operating costs would be reduced by 10 percent. "No mean feat for a third-generation derivative based on an airframe designed nearly 20 years ago," said Joe Sutter in 1986.

The winglets were made of lightweight composite materials, which also featured heavily in other areas of the airframe along with a new series of advanced aluminum alloys. Canted outward at 29 degrees and swept back at 60

degrees, the 6-foot-tall carbon fiber devices reduced drag and improved cruise performance to produce a 3-percent increase in range. Other aerodynamic-related changes included a recontoured wing to body fairing and the addition of an extra (11th) leading-edge wing flap. Each wing tip was also extended by 6 feet to grow the wingspan to 211 feet. When the aircraft was fully fueled, the extra weight bent the winglets outwards by an extra foot, temporarily growing the span to 213 feet! Extra space for fuel was also provided for a 3,300-gallon tank in the horizontal stabilizer.

Most of the major internal changes were concentrated in the flight deck, which was radically modernized to bring it up to the two-crew standards of the 757 and 767 (see chapter 7). Dominated by a six-tube glass cockpit display system, the flight deck had 365 lights, gauges, and switches, or roughly only a third of those found in the three-crew "classic" 747. The digital flight deck allowed the introduction of more automated and streamlined procedures. To deal with an engine fire, for example, a "classic" crew checked off 15 items compared to just four on the -400. Other advances included a central maintenance computer, which helped engineers troubleshoot problems and bring them to the attention of maintenance staff before any human operator would have noticed a problem. Others were a more sophisticated flight-management computer that was five times faster than its predecessor and able to compute "4D" navigation. This is a calculation of whether or not an aircraft could reach a particular altitude by a certain navigational waypoint.

The changes in the flight deck were mirrored by a radical revision of the interior, which was all new. Everything was different from the shaping and materials of the cabin walls to the lavatory system and overhead bins. It was the complexities of the new cabin as well as the flight deck avionics that began to spell trouble for the -400 program.

Boeing had effectively bitten off more than it could chew and the -400 development began to suffer delays. First flight slipped a month to April 29, 1988 and software and production problems caused more delays to the test program. By 1989 the bulk of the problems had been overcome, however, and international services commenced with Singapore Airlines to London on May 30 and Northwest flew the first -400 service the following day between New York and Tokyo.

Although suffering from more than its fair share of teething problems, the -400 went on to become the best selling 747 variant. As with earlier versions, the -400 family quickly grew to encompass combis, domestics, and freighters—the latter providing capacity for up to 124 tons of cargo, and up to 26 more tons than the 747-200F. By 1998 more than 550 -400s had been ordered, a fifth of which were either pure freighters or combis. The 747 meanwhile continued to provide the bread-and-butter income the company needed to continue its expansion. On April 23, 1998, a 747-400 became the 2,000th Seattle-built widebody (including 767s and 777s) to be rolled out. At the time Boeing worked out that during its lifetime, the 747 fleet had logged more than 50 million flight hours, 12 million flights, and 20 billion miles—or enough to make 42,000 trips to the moon and back!

An Uzbekistan 767-300 looms large in the lens on finals. Note the forward sloping undercarriage bogies and the retractable tail skid. The four-wheel main bogie is positioned to enable it to fit snugly into the undercarriage bay.

7

High-Tech Twins

The 747 was a hard act to follow, even for Boeing. Yet in 1978 the company set itself the unprecedented task of developing two completely new and very different jetliners at virtually the same time. In spite of the fact that each incorporated radical advances in avionics, systems, and aerodynamic design, both were expected to fly within four years of launch and within almost four months of each other.

Before applauding Boeing for its courage and iron will, it must be realized that the challenge arose more by accident than design. The company readily admitted it would have preferred to spread the development cost and risk of both types, dubbed the 757 and 767, over a longer period by producing the pair in series rather than in parallel. However, the situation was forced on the company. The long-looked-for market upturn finally happened in 1978 and carried the new programs with it. Both had been under study, in various guises, for more than six years by then, and the timing of the two independent efforts meshed with rising airline interest. This forced them to coexist and, ultimately, to be treated as almost one program even though the 767 actually led the 757 by about nine months.

The result was a pair of "new generation" aircraft quite unlike anything produced from the Boeing stable before. Neither aircraft had any of the classic design hallmarks that had distinguished Boeing jetliners from the 707. Gone, for example, was the sharply pointed, snake-like nose section and distinctive angular flight deck of the 707, 727, and 737. Also absent was the sharply swept wing and four-engine configuration, which instantly proclaimed the shared heritage of the 707 and 747.

Instead, the appearance of the snub-nosed 757 shocked the industry. Most expected to see a smaller widebody, as narrowbodies were considered distinctly out of vogue. By contrast, the rather squat, bulky 767 had an unusual "semi-widebody" cross-section that was unique to the industry.

The differences were even more radical inside. The "steam" or "clockwork" cockpits of the previous generation were replaced by advanced digital flight decks with "glass" TV displays, and computerized systems took the place of the trusty and once indispensable flight engineer. The two were truly unique—the first of Boeing's new generation. So where did they come from and what heritage, if any, did they share with their Boeing predecessors?

757—NEW-LOOK NARROWBODY

The tangled roots of the 757 are difficult to trace. The sprightly jetliner did not appear suddenly on the airline scene in the early 1980s ready to fill the place of the 727 and carve other niches for itself. Instead, it emerged painfully slow from

The Boeing-owned 757 prototype was used by Military Airplanes division as a flying testbed for the avionics of the Lockheed Martin-Boeing F-22 Raptor fighter. The nose, seen here, was fitted with the F-22's AN/APG-77 radar while the crown of the fuselage above the flight deck was later modified to house a representative F-22 wing section. This was also crammed with conformal sensors and antennae and earned the 757 the nickname "Catfish."

The birth of the 757 followed the death of 727-derivative studies like these. United Airlines was particularly interested in the 727-300 stretch (closest to the camera). Lengthened by 18 feet, 4 inches, the -300 incorporated a wider-span wing and newer 20,850-pound-thrust engines. Another widebody 727 derivative was never launched, but the cross-section was adopted for the 7X7 program, which eventually became the 767.

a melting pot of studies going back over years. To make matters even more confusing, the same broth also produced the 767.

Like any manufacturer, Boeing hoped to maintain market lead with a simple, relatively inexpensive derivative rather than face the enormous cost of an all-new design. This was particularly true at a time when the market was weak and rising fuel prices were adding to the uncertainty. The logical approach was therefore to study new versions of the 727-200, which, by the early 1970s was showing promising signs of becoming the best-selling jetliner in history.

It is not surprising that Boeing, in close cooperation with its trusty customer United Airlines, came up with the 727-300. Compared with the -200, it featured a 220-inch fuselage stretch, adding 30 to 40 passengers, a new landing gear, redesigned wing leading edge, a 6-foot increase in span, and 20,850-pound-thrust P&W JT8D-217 turbofans. All-up weight by the time of the 1975 Paris air show was expected to be around 222,0000 pounds.

United looked set to order the 727-300 into production when events suddenly conspired to kill the program in the fall of that year. Boeing veteran designer Jack Steiner was convinced that he was partly to blame. "757 evolution was interesting, and I guess I was involved more than I really wanted to be," said Steiner

in a talk to Boeing retirees in 1991. Steiner was running an advanced development program called the 7X7, which, as explained below, became the 767. Although the 7X7 ultimately evolved into a larger aircraft, it embodied all the new technology also feeding into another design project that was at an even more embryonic stage, the 7N7. This included new, second-generation high-bypass-ratio turbofans, advanced composites and other lightweight structures, better aerodynamics and uprated systems, and flight deck technology.

Steiner worked closely with Dick Ferris of United Airlines, who was leading the airline's purchase of the -300. Ferris wanted to "check out on every airplane we flew, and a lot of other things," Steiner recalled. "So he was out in the factory, and I collared him. This was just before the -300 was going to be announced. So I put him in the office, and I showed him what the 'X7' technology was like, and, of course, it was very apparent that the 'X7' was a different generation from the '27-300. And that ended the '27-300. He went back home and called up Boeing and said he wasn't interested. I'm afraid I precipitated that myself."

As with so many similar serendipitous events in Boeing history, the -300 cancellation was to prove fortuitous. The aircraft was, at best, an interim solution and by dying young it cleared the way for the 757, which was in a different class competitively. As for United, it would go on to operate a huge fleet of more than 100 757s by 1998. Ironically, the cancellation of the 727-300 was probably good news for Airbus Industrie, which was struggling hard to sell the A300B in the mid-1970s. Sales of the European short-haul jetliner would have been hit hard by the launch of the -300, as many of the early customers were also 727 operators and may well have chosen commonality over the relatively untried widebody.

Yet the 727 derivative was not quite dead. As late as 1977 Braniff Airlines breathed new life into the aircraft when it announced a requirement for a 170-seater. Braniff, which was still a big influence in the business before the onslaught of deregulation in the U.S. airline industry, enticed Boeing by saying it would need up to 150 to replace its 727s and build up its fleet. The response was a "stretched 727" with seating for 162 and two new high-bypass-ratio engines. The choice was between General Electric's proposed CF6-32, Pratt & Whitney's JT10-4, and Rolls-Royce's "cropped fan" RB.211-535. Over the course of the year the plans changed. The aircraft grew

slightly in size and gradually became identified with a new designation, the 7N7.

The original base-line configuration of the 7N7 was attributed to product development director Bob Norton. Steiner, in fact, believed the "N" stood for Norton. "Norton came up with this smaller airplane that was pretty attractive," he said. "It looked like the '57 looks now, but it was a lot smaller." He added that the 757 was "a direct descendant of the '27, and it got to the point where it was an all-new airplane except for the cockpit, and, of course, later on we made that new, too." The principal aim of the 7N7 and 7X7 was to capture the new advances in technology that were just becoming available to the aerospace community. The driver was the explosion in fuel costs that had followed the Yom Kippur Middle East war of 1973

and sent the global economy and its airlines into a tailspin. When the war began, jet fuel cost $0.11 per U.S. gallon. One year later it had skyrocketed to $1.10.

From the very start the focus of the 7N7 was therefore on efficiency. Taken as a whole, Boeing estimated two of the new generation turbofans would offer fuel savings of roughly 20 percent and that aerodynamic and weight-saving improvements could be worth another 10 percent. Even the decision to stick with the familiar six-abreast fuselage section of the 727 was largely based on drag considerations. By staying narrowbody, Boeing estimated it would save 7 percent in fuel costs over a seven-abreast section. Compared to the similarly sized 707-120, which was also a transcontinental range aircraft, the fuel burn per seat-mile of the 757 would eventually turn out to be 42 percent

The first production 757, built for the launch customer Eastern Airlines, now flies as a research aircraft for NASA Langley. The aircraft was in storage at Las Vegas for three years before NASA acquired it in 1994. It is reported that engineers discovered a quantity of cocaine hidden aboard it when the aircraft was refurbished.

145

An
Avianca Columbia aircraft, leased from GPA, approaches Los Angeles from Bogota's El Dorado airport. Like many operators, Avianca selected the Rolls-Royce-powered RB.211-535E4 version, which was leased from GPA.

The
world's only 757 Combi approaches Kai Tak in-bound from Kathmandu. The Rolls-Royce RB.211-535E4-powered 757-2F8 Combi was selected by Royal Air Nepal for its mixed passenger/freight loads out of Tribhuvan airfield in the foothills of the Himalayas. The aircraft can accommodate two 88x108-inch pallets as well as 164 passengers.

lower! Even next to the comparatively efficient 727-200, the new aircraft would burn 40 percent less fuel per seat on a 1,000-nautical-mile trip.

Further refinements to save weight, and therefore fuel consumption, included the extensive use of new composite materials and improved aluminum alloys. Taken together, Boeing hoped to make the advanced aircraft about 2,000 pounds lighter than an identically sized jetliner of the previous generation. Assuming the aircraft would make around 1,400 trips of about 1,000 nautical miles in length, the company worked out that the weight saving alone would save up to 30,000 U.S. gallons a year.

In fact, the design was optimized early on for stage lengths of 500 nautical miles and typical sector flying times of less than 2 hours. As passengers rather than freight were expected to be the priority of this short-range market, the narrowbody's reduced underfloor cargo capacity was not considered to be a big factor. Boeing's market research also supported the narrowbody decision. It showed that passengers apparently chose a widebody over a narrowbody on flights of more than a couple of hours but not for shorter journeys.

By 1978 the 7N7 concept began to firm up into two family members. The first was a shortbody -100 with seats in a typical mixed-class arrangement for around 160. The second version, dubbed the -200, was about 100 inches longer with seating for around 180. At this stage the aircraft still featured a slimmed down, aerodynamically refined version of the 727 high tail unit as well as the trijet's forward fuselage and flight deck.

One of the first major design departures from the 727 was the wing. Two engines were better for fuel economy, and following the logic of the 737, it made sense to relieve bending moment by hanging them on the wing rather than grouping them by the tail. Another big design driver was the careful focus on mission requirements. Unlike the 727, which was designed for high performance in the 1960s, the 7N7 was aimed specifically at the economically minded short-haul routes where speed was less vital. Boeing calculated that climb consumed 60 percent of the fuel that the 7N7 would use on a 500-nautical-mile trip. It was therefore expected to spend almost as much time climbing and descending as cruising. As a result, the wing was optimized for a Mach 0.8 cruise, substantially less than the 727's Mach 0.9 top speed.

This brand-new 757 bound for Turkmenistan is prepared for its first flight at Renton in August 1996. The opening up of the former Soviet Union countries provided new opportunities for Boeing, which saw increased sales of 737s, 757s, 767s, and even 777s as a result.

Double-slotted flaps and full-span slats are responsible for the 757's excellent short-field capabilities. Here a British Airways 757 in the airline's controversial late 1990s livery approaches London Heathrow. The tall main gear legs, also evident in this view, were designed in from the start to easily allow the 757 to be stretched.

The 7N7 aerofoil was no ordinary wing but, together with the very similar 7X7 aerofoil, represented Boeing's first use of "aft-loaded" design technology. This meant the wing had a comparatively flat top and a small undersurface cusp near the trailing edge. The aft-loaded wing produced the same benefits as the virtually identical super-critical section, namely a reduced wing sweep, an efficient structure, and delayed Mach drag-rise. The shape produced lift across more of the upper surface instead of a relatively narrow area close behind the leading edge. As a result, the air was accelerated more gradually across the upper surface instead of rapidly speeding up to supersonic velocity and creating a drag-inducing shock wave.

With all these factors in mind, designers, therefore, set the wing sweep at a relatively modest 25 degrees at quarter-chord, compared to the 727's rakish 32 degrees. The lower sweep could be tolerated without much drag penalty because of the aircraft's lower average speed, and it allowed Boeing to dispense with the complexity of inboard ailerons. Although the span was larger than the 727, which also helped reduce induced drag on the 757, the reduced sweep meant the structure was stiffer. As aircraft speed and sweep had increased, designers discovered that flexible wing structures were prone to aileron reversal. This meant that at high speeds the aerodynamic loads distorted the outer wing structure, rendering the ailerons useless for

controlling the aircraft. As a result, inboard ailerons were built onto the trailing edge nearer the body, where the wing was stiffer. They worked well but added weight and systems complexity and reduced efficiency.

Another outstanding feature of the 757 wing was an impressive array of high-lift devices packaged carefully into low-drag housings. Large, double-slotted flaps operated by a track and carriage were designed for the

Boeing developed a special -200PF (Package Freighter) version for United Parcel Service. The aircraft is identical to a high-gross-weight, 250,000-pound passenger aircraft, but all passenger services, windows, and entry doors are deleted. A large 134x86.5-inch cargo door is installed in the left side of the forward fuselage, together with a new crew entry door. The 757PF can accommodate up to 15 pallets on the main deck, with extra space in the belly holds.

Private 757s have been developed, one of which is used by local Seattle-based billionaire and Microsoft cofounder Paul Allen. The aircraft is fitted with a pioneering roof-mounted antenna capable of receiving direct TV satellite signals.

The USAF adopted the 757 to replace its VIP VC-137 transports. The first of four C-32As, as they were designated, flew for the first time in February 1998 and is seen here in the final stages of assembly the previous November. The aircraft was delivered to the 89th Airlift Wing at Andrews AFB, Maryland, from where it was used to carry the U.S. vice president, cabinet members, and members of Congress traveling on government business.

trailing-edge, and full-span slats were fitted to the leading edge. In terms of sophistication, the flaps owed as much to the 747 as the 727.

The wing root was also wide, enabling easy stowage of the twin bogied undercarriage. Although the truck design was very similar to the 707, the legs were much longer—for several reasons. One was ground clearance for the high-bypass-ratio engines, which had fan diameters of almost 80 inches, more than double that of the JT8D versions powering the 727. New engines on offer included the RB.211-535, the CF6-32, and P&W JT10D, the latter eventually becoming the PW2000.

The deep-root section, added to the 5-degree dihedral of the wing, also necessitated a long leg. Another rea-

son, and one that ironically did not begin to pay dividends until almost 20 years after its launch, was the extra margin to stretch the fuselage. Boeing Chairman and Chief Executive Phil Condit was chief engineer on the 757 and recalled in a 1991 interview that pioneering Boeing designer Ed Wells had been partially responsible for the 757's tall gear. Condit remembered Wells attending a configuration meeting and saying, ". . . you know, on the 707, we made the landing gear as short as we could because of weight, and when Douglas stretched the DC-8, we couldn't stretch the 707 because the gear was too short. I know it costs some weight, but if I were you, I'd consider seriously leaving yourselves some room." Condit added, "That's why the landing gear on the '57 is the length it is."

At
a very late stage the 767 design, still
known at the time as the 7X7,
sported a T-tail based on that of the
727. By adopting a low tail, Boeing
was able to maximize passenger
load without increasing fuselage
length and avoided any possibility of
running into deep-stall problems.

The
757 and 767 share identical cockpits to
reduce crew training costs and simplify
scheduling. Boeing chose the moment
to introduce new computer-driven,
cathode ray tube-based TV displays
and an associated new display
philosophy. The flight deck features
revolutionized Boeing's future cockpit
designs and had a direct influence on
the configuration of the 747-400, the
updated 737-300/400/500 Series, and
the 777. In this photograph of a
757-200 simulator, the crew is on finals
to London Gatwick with the number
two engine failed.

Input from another Boeing pioneer, Ken Holtby, also
eliminated the T-tail from the design more than a year after
British Airways and Eastern Airlines announced their
intent to order the 757. Condit said, ". . . we will not have
airplanes that have locked-in stall. As you stall the airplane,
if the wake of the wing or the engines covers the horizontal, it doesn't matter what you do with the elevator, you're
in. 'Locked-in' is if you don't have enough elevator power
to drive yourself back out." Two British-built T-tail contemporaries of the 727, the British Aircraft Corporation
BAC 1-11 and Hawker Siddeley HS.121 Trident, both
suffered losses due to "locked-in stall" or "super stall."
These problems were cured by the use of "stick pushers,"
which automatically activated the control column and
forced the aircraft's nose down before the stall was unre-

These two pictures perfectly illustrate the differences between the base-line 767-200 and the stretched -300 (below). The American Airlines 767-200 is 159 feet, 2 inches in overall length, whereas the Delta Airlines 767-300 has been stretched to 180 feet, 3 inches by the insertion of a 121-inch plug forward of the wing and a 132-inch section aft. The wingspan and vertical and horizontal tail surfaces are identical.

coverable, but it reinforced Boeing's decision to stick with body-mounted stabilizers on its next design. The late change to the low tail also allowed the aircraft's overall length to be decreased by 18 feet, 8 inches—from 172 feet, 9 inches to 155 feet, 3 inches, while the internal dimensions of the cabin remained basically unaltered.

Other changes in and beneath the skin took the 757 even further from the 727 design. A large amount of composites, some 3,340 pounds in all, were used in the new twin to save around 1,490 pounds. Carbon-fiber-reinforced plastic (CFRP) was used for elevators, rudder, ailerons, spoilers, and engine cowls while Kevlar was used extensively for most access panels, undercarriage doors, and wing/fuselage and flap-track fairings. Kevlar-reinforced plastic was also used for panels, pylon, fin, and tailplane tip fairings. Up to 11,380 pounds of improved aluminum alloys, with between 5 and 13 percent higher strength, were also used in the design. In addition to saving more than 600 pounds through the better aluminum alloys, Boeing also shaved a further 1,500 pounds through a three-year-long weight-saving program.

Systems and internal configuration design also reflected the shift away from the 727. With only the fuselage cross-section now remaining as the last feature common to the older trijet, Boeing did everything possible to disguise this fact from the inside. A new "widebody look" interior was designed with carefully contoured side panels and clever lighting to create a feeling of spaciousness. Revised overhead baggage bins were twice the capacity of the 727 bins, and for the first time, emergency lighting was built into the lower lip of the bins instead of into the ceiling. Other changes from the 727 included chemical generators for emergency oxygen, door escape slides, which double as rafts (derived from the 747), and an improved air-conditioning system. Two Garrett AiResearch (now AlliedSignal) air conditioners fed the cabin with an equal mix of fresh air and recirculated, filtered air. Until this point, air conditioners had traditionally been fresh air only, a practice that was more expensive in bleed-air and hence fuel burn.

More late changes were fed into the design at a surprisingly late stage. Other than the move to the low tail, the biggest external change was the adoption of a blunter, rounded nose and redesigned flight deck. This more closely matched that of the 767 (see below) and profoundly altered the overall look of the new Boeing jetliner.

Production go-ahead was finally given in March 1979 after the two launch airlines had signed on the dotted line for a total of 40 firm orders. Both selected the Rolls-Royce RB.211-535C engine, making it the first Boeing jetliner ever to be launched with a non-U.S. engine. In November 1980 the program received a major boost when Delta placed a record order for 60 aircraft to be powered by the Pratt & Whitney PW2037, sparking off the beginning of a fierce rivalry between the two engine makers. Final assembly of the first aircraft began three months later, and on January 13, 1982, the first aircraft (N757A) was rolled out at Renton.

767—FLEXIBLE WIDEBODY

With no obvious links between the all-new 767 design and any of its Boeing predecessors, the 767's complex genealogy requires some detective work. Strangely, at least part of the trail begins in the early 1970s in Renton, home of the narrowbodies, rather than Everett, where all Boeing widebody work is concentrated.

Swissair was searching for a high-capacity, short- to medium-haul airliner for its European trunk routes, and Boeing's most successful salesman, Tex Bouillion, believed the niche could be filled by a widebody version of the 727. Jack Steiner, who was vice president and general manager of 707/727/737 programs at Renton during the difficult early 1970s, recalled, "I had been told by Tex that if I could sell a widebody 727 to Swissair, we'd build it. I went over to Swissair, and that's how the 727XX got born. We made a mockup of it, and I know a bunch of people at Everett called it the 727 double cross."

The 727XX did not survive, and Swissair ultimately bought the Airbus A310, the direct competitor of what was to become the 767. However, the fuselage of the 727XX was an interesting twin-aisle design, which was very close to the cross-section eventually adopted for the 767. Steiner confirms the lineage, saying the mockup, which was essentially a 727 nose section grafted onto a bulging fuselage measuring around 16 feet in diameter, was "swiped by [Ken] Holtby for the 7X7, which I inherited when I became head of the 7X7. So you know, life is kind of funny."

Boeing formed the 7X7 organization in 1972, headed by Vice President and General Manager Ken Holtby, to "determine the definition of the next product offering and to develop a family relationship of that product, ranging from short-haul to long-haul market application," said

NEXT
A perfect display of the 767's single-slotted outboard and double-slotted inboard trailing-edge flaps is provided by this Vietnam Airlines -300 as it turns onto finals at Hong Kong's Kai Tak.

Boeing at the time. "Present plans are based on entering the intermediate market through a joint venture with Aeritalia. Other joint ventures for short-range and long-range versions are also possible." Holtby toured the world discussing the 7X7 with airlines, but by the end of 1972 the project was still highly uncertain. Boeing knew it wanted something larger than a 707 but smaller than a 747 and the other widebodies, the A300, DC-10, and L-1011. It sketched out a preliminary "semi-widebody" design in September of that year. Despite being six years from go-ahead, it already shared some remarkable similarities with what would eventually become the 767. Its fuselage diameter, one of the hardest issues to resolve in modern airliner design, was 188 inches, only 10 inches shy of the final design. Its length was 159 feet, a mere 2 inches short of the final length adopted for the initial -200 version.

The joint venture with Aeritalia and a similar agreement with Japan were significant departures for Boeing, which saw two main reasons for the partnerships. First, they helped spread the huge costs of development, which could no longer be supported by a single company. Second, they encouraged sales to the partner's national and regional marketplace. The 7X7, and therefore the 767, was Boeing's first major international development program. The original plan with Aeritalia was a 50-50 development of a program code-named the BA.751/7X7. At this stage the 7X7 was an advanced short takeoff and landing (STOL), short-range airliner dubbed the quiet, short haul (QSH). Two years later, in 1974, the 7X7 was evolving

into a transcontinental-range airliner, and the Italian share had dropped to 20 percent. However, with an estimated development price tag of $1 billion, Aeritalia's managing director at the time, Dr. Ernesto Postiglioni, noted that "20 percent of that is a lot of money."

Aeritalia's early involvement paid dividends. In August 1978, one year after the formal launch of the 767, it signed up as a risk-sharing participant in the program. It later merged with Selenia and was known as Alenia. This company, now part of the Finmeccanica group, went on to be responsible for the 767 wing control surfaces, flaps, leading-edge slats, wing tips, elevators, fin, rudder, and nose radome.

Japan's early involvement was tied initially to a separate short-range 150-seat jet study called the YX. As these studies dragged on inconclusively for years, the YX and 7X7 efforts gradually fused, enabling Japan's Civil Transport Development Corporation a chance to get involved in the larger program. CTDC, which later become known as the Commercial Airplane Company, was made up of Fuji, Kawasaki, and Mitsubishi Heavy Industries. Their consistent eagerness to become involved also paid off when the CDTC signed a risk-sharing partnership deal on September 22, 1978, under which the Japanese companies would supply virtually the entire 767 fuselage. Under the agreement, Fuji supplied wing fairings and main gear doors; Kawasaki, center fuselage body panels, exit hatches, and wing in-spar ribs; while Mitsubishi provided the rear fuselage body panels, passenger and cargo doors, stringers, and the dorsal fin.

TAKING SHAPE

Boeing's studies of the QSH with Aeritalia fizzled out because of airline apathy, and attention was switched to a larger aircraft with seating for between 180 and 200 and a range of almost 2,000 nautical miles. This study, dubbed the IRA (intermediate-range aircraft), sat between the A300B2 and the 727-200 and represented the middle ground between the 7X7 and the later 7N7 projects. Two further derivatives were sketched out, which seemed to make a lot of sense. One was a longer range, transcontinental IRA with the same capacity but 1,000 nautical miles more range. Another was a much longer range, intercontinental version that would provide an improved replacement for the 707-320B and DC-8-62 but suit the longer, thinner routes, which could not support the DC-10-30 and 747.

The blueprint slowly emerged from this to reveal two basic designs by early 1973: a twin-engined 7X7 for the short and medium routes and a trijet for the long-haul sectors. The earliest versions of the twinjet featured overwing engines with blown flaps inherited from the QSH study, a configuration that quickly dropped out of the picture with increasing aircraft size. Later versions were configured with high-bypass-ratio turbofans, such as the CF6, JT9D, or RB.211, hung underwing in the standard manner.

Within two years the picture was transformed yet again, thanks mainly to critical breakthroughs in engine and aerofoil technology. After more than 1,000 hours of wind-tunnel testing of more than 100 designs, Boeing had honed the basic 7X7 down to two main versions. Revealing its latest plans at the 1975 Paris air show, Boeing showed plans for two trijets powered by the new generation of 10-ton turbofans. The choice lay between the General Electric/Snecma CFM56, which was under development for certification in 1977 and the 25,000-pound-thrust version of the Pratt & Whitney JT10. An engine of this size eventually emerged as the International Aero Engines V2500 in a partnership with Rolls-Royce, Fiat Avio, MTU, and Japanese Aero Engines (a consortium of Ishikawajima-Harima, Kawasaki, and Mitsubishi Heavy Industries). The 38,000-pound-thrust JT10D-4, proposed for the 7N7 (see above), eventually became the PW2000.

Throughout this whole period the two dominant design drivers of the 7X7 remained noise and fuel consumption. The wing design, using an advanced new cross-section, was expected to offer an 8-percent fuel saving and made it possible to use an engine 13 percent smaller than

would have been the case with a conventional wing. Fuel burn per passenger was expected to be around 118 pounds over a 1,000-nautical-mile sector, compared to 166 pounds for the 727-200ADV.

The two proposed variants included a 200-seat basic model for the U.S. domestic market and a smaller 175-seater aimed at a European trunkliner requirement from Air France, Lufthansa, and British Airways. Critically, two key characteristics of the definitive 767 crystallized at this point: The fuselage width was established at 16 feet, 6 inches (198 inches), and the U.S. domestic version empty weight was estimated at 167,000 pounds (the basic empty weight of the 767-200 is 164,800 pounds).

Boeing created more wing area, and therefore room for future growth, when it spread the kink-point of the trailing edge farther outboard to house the wide-spaced main gear. This, in turn, followed Boeing's decision to adopt a relatively narrow, high-aspect-ratio wing.

The prototype 767 now sports this unusual canoe-shaped fairing on the fuselage roof. This houses sophisticated infrared and other devices to track ballistic missiles and similar objects in flight. The Airborne Surveillance Testbed was formerly called the Airborne Optical Adjunct when it was first developed to support the U.S. Department of Defense's Star Wars Initiative.

More than 25 airlines were contacted for their input during 1974 and 1975, representing Boeing's first tentative steps toward embracing full customer involvement in later designs like the 777. The company built a mockup embodying all its ideas, which showed a five- or six-abreast layout in first class and seven abreast in economy. In all charter configurations, up to eight abreast could be fitted.

Unlike the 747, the 7X7 body was designed to cater to the "people market rather than the freighter market," said Steiner. The major drawback of the cross-section was an inability to carry two LD-3 freight containers back-to-back in the lower lobe. The LD-3 had become the standard con-

tainer, but Boeing gambled that a specially designed smaller container would be widely adopted, particularly by U.S. carriers, for the 767 fleet. Boeing originally designated the new container the LD-3A, but feared it sounded like a compromise. The container was rechristened the LD67 for a while before ultimately becoming the LD-2 of today.

Encouraging research showed a total market for around 1,000 aircraft in its class over the next 20 years, including 500 in the United States and 250 in Europe. But 1975 was to prove a slack year for demand, and the project dragged on into 1976 with major arguments raging over such basic design features as whether the 7X7 should be a twin or a trijet. The choice was still driven by the airlines. United, with its high-altitude yardstick of a hot and high takeoff from Denver, favored three engines. Delta and Western, with slightly less-demanding requirements, opted for the fuel efficiency of a twin.

In 1976 Boeing's 7X7 configuration group held a stormy meeting that effectively decided the future of the 767. Steiner regarded it as the "harshest meeting that I ever remember on a top-of-the-corporation scale. That was the meeting in which I had been running the program with 'number one' as a three-engine airplane and 'number two' as a two-engine airplane. And Schairer and Wells came over to our room in the 10-60 building, and they said, [for] over an hour, while many of us got smaller and smaller and wetter and wetter, 'You're backwards. The "number one" airplane's got to be the twin and the "number two's" the trijet.' And of course, they won. They were paying our salaries."

The input was decisive. Schairer and Wells recognized two significant points: the indisputable economy of twins versus trijets and the growing reliability of the second generation turbofans. By the mid-1970s the cost of fuel had mushroomed to about a half of direct operating cost. One fewer engine also saved weight, and with no long over-water requirement foreseen, this third engine proved inessential. Ironically, the 767 would go on to usher in the age of long-range over-water flights, or extended-range twin-engined operations (ETOPS). This phenomenon would dramatically alter the face of the air transport industry in the 1980s and 1990s as well as profoundly influence Boeing's future designs and even those of their competitors.

Two years later the 7X7 was finally firm enough to be given the model number 767, yet incredibly the trijet version remained an option until very late in the development as two separate design groups performed back-to-back analysis of the twin and trijet concepts. Boeing outlined three versions of the aircraft, two twins and a trijet. The 767-100 was offered as a 180–190-seat medium hauler with a maximum takeoff weight of 237,100 pounds. The larger -200 was offered with seats for up to 210 and a maximum weight of between 287,100 and 294,600 pounds. Finally, the trijet version, designated the 767MR/LR, was a 200-seater with an intercontinental range.

GO-AHEAD

As always, events were ultimately dictated by the airlines and not the marketers. On July 14, 1978, the 767 was finally launched into production by United Airlines, which ordered 30 series -200s powered by Pratt & Whitney JT9D-7R4Ds. Later that month the European A310, arch rival of the 767, was also launched on the back of commitments from Air France, Lufthansa, and Swissair. The race was on.

Boeing said the 767 launch "climaxed several years of unprecedented airplane development activity. Never before in the company's history has a new airplane been so thoroughly studied, analyzed, and wind-tunnel tested prior to production go-ahead." By April 1981 more than 26,000 hours of wind-tunnel work had been amassed, compared with 14,000 hours for the 747 and 4,000 hours for the 727. Market size at launch was estimated at around 1,500.

New orders quickly rolled in from American and Delta, which together placed orders for 50 and options on 42 more. Both chose the GE CF6-80A to power their aircraft, marking the significant fact that the 767 was the first Boeing jetliner launched with a choice of two engines. By the end of 1978 orders from four airlines stood at 84, all of which were for the -200. Nobody was interested in the -100, which nudged dangerously close in size to the 757-200, and the option was quietly dropped. The 767MR/LR, by now designated 777, was meanwhile delayed. Eventually, this too was dropped in favor of a heavier, long-range version of the -200, which was to become an "extended range" or -200ER.

Construction of parts for the first 767 began on July 6, 1979, and the final assembly of the development aircraft, appropriately registered N767BA, started in April 1981. The outside world got its first real look at the big, new twin a few months later when it was rolled out of the big Everett assembly site doors on August 4, 1981.

At first glance, the main impression was created by the big, 156-foot, 1-inch wingspan. With a relatively huge area of 3,050 square feet, the wing had a high aspect ratio of 7.98 and looked perfect for sustained long-range cruise. Boeing naturally used its newly perfected aft-loaded aerofoil technology to increase wing thickness without drag penalty. The thicker section allowed an efficient structure for the large span and, importantly, ensured plenty of room for fuel. Thickness/chord ratio was 10.5 percent at the tip and gradually increased to 15 percent at the root.

The wing area was slightly larger than strictly necessary because of the need to accommodate the well-spaced undercarriage. It is the need to house the main gear that gives swept wings their traditional trailing-edge kink near the fuselage. By adopting a relatively narrow, high-aspect-

ratio wing, Boeing, therefore, needed to push the kink point out slightly farther, creating more wing area near the root. At first this seemed to be dead weight, but in reality it gave the 767 vital room from future growth and the ability to cruise higher.

The wing was also swept at 31.5 degrees at a quarter chord, or just 0.5 degrees shy of the arrowlike 727 planform. However, the reasons were quite different. The 727 wing called for reasonable lift at low speed without excessive cruise drag, whereas the 767 had the maximum span possible with its undercarriage location and a relatively slower Mach 0.8 cruise. The design also provided one of the best elliptical spanwise distributions of lift ever achieved on a Boeing airliner. The designers also produced a similar result on the tailplane by introducing washout for the first time along the span.

Another instantly observable feature was the low tailplane. Artist impressions at the time of the launch in July 1978 depicted it with a T-tail, and the feature survived until late in the final design phase. Ed Wells was again influential in the decision to go for the low tail, which allowed Boeing to maximize passenger load without increasing aircraft length, thereby letting the 767 use the same airport ramp space as other medium-range airliners. The unusual, seven-abreast cross-section was also related to length as this allowed Boeing to taper the rear fuselage in a shorter length. The same feature also enabled the passenger cabin to have parallel walls along its entire length. This avoided the wasted space of off-seat rows and gave more interior flexibility. Boe-

ing also claimed it gave the 767 up to 30 percent more cargo volume than the A310, despite admitting the need for the special LD-2 containers. Critically, the new cross-section meant that the 767 had to be more than 80 percent full before the deeply unpopular middle-row center seats had to be occupied—a major lesson from the company's market research over the previous years.

The 767's big engines, each capable of developing more than 21 tons of thrust, were mounted closer to the wing than those of the 747. This was to keep the undercarriage relatively short and to ensure that asymmetric thrust would be minimized in the event of an engine failure. The engine struts were short and wider than earlier designs, which had been deeper. The strut was attached to the wing in five places and weak links ensured that in the event of a wheels-up landing, the engine and strut would simply tip upwards. This ensured the engine would stay attached to the wing and lessen the chance of rupturing fuel tanks.

COMMON COCKPIT

The hallmark of the 757/767 was the 1979 decision to opt for identical cockpits and flying qualities. At first glance, it looked an impossible task, after all the 757 and 767 were completely different in size and weight. However, Boeing had managed something similar with the 747 and 747SP (see chapter 6) and believed the benefits of attempting it on the new generation would be enormous.

One obvious advantage was a common type rating, which would reduce crew training, simplify scheduling, and allow airlines flying both types to operate a common seniority roster. The use of common instrumentation, avionics, and systems would also reduce the cost and time of development and certification.

The key to achieving the goal was the availability of new digital avionics and cathode ray tube (CRT) displays. These mini-TV-like screens were totally flexible, as the computers driving them could be programmed to display almost anything, including complex engine information that normally preoccupied the flight engineer at a dedicated cockpit station. The new-look "glass cockpit" was therefore designed for two crew, though initial versions of the 767 were offered (and built) with provisions for a flight engineer. Only later, after a U.S. Presidential "task force" review of safety of two-crew airline operations, was the base-line design altered.

Six Rockwell Collins CRTs were in the standard cockpit—two electronic flight instrumentation system (EFIS) displays for each pilot and a shared pair of engine indication and crew alerting (EICAS) displays. EFIS replaced each pilot's traditional "steam" electromechanical attitude director indicator and horizontal situation indicator. EICAS replaced engine monitoring instruments and gave an extra dimension to caution and warning messages. EICAS could also be used to check the status of various aircraft systems, such as hydraulics, and could be used like an electronic flight manual.

The sheer variety and adaptability of the new displays gave Boeing some headaches during development. It had to be careful not to overwhelm the crew with unnecessary detail and yet ensure that no vital but small detail was omitted. CRT symbology was also carefully defined after prolonged consultation with pilots.

As the automated systems had taken the role of the flight engineer, Boeing put a lot of emphasis on automatic switchover in the event of a system failure. It also did a lot to simplify systems management so that, even without the flight engineer, the crew workload was reduced, not increased.

One of the biggest single reductions in workload was achieved with the adoption of a fully integrated Sperry (now Honeywell) flight management system (FMS). This was a first for the common cockpit and formed the real "brain" of the aircraft by linking the air-data computer, autopilot, internal-reference navigation system, other navigation aids, thrust-management computer, and caution/warning system. It allowed navigation, performance management and automatic flight to be controlled through a single unit, drastically cutting down pilot workload.

Attitude data was supplied by three Honeywell laser-gyros mounted directly on the airframe. Each unit sensed angular accelerations, which were integrated into attitude and position. The 757 and 767 were the first airliners to be equipped with laser-based attitude and heading reference system (AHRS) gyros.

The common cockpit also had to physically fit both airframes, and Boeing achieved this with a clever geometric compromise. On the 757 the cockpit was grafted onto the fuselage with a step down and a 2-degree floor slope. On the 767 this was achieved with a step up. Both aircraft were fitted with the same front two windows, an arrangement that ensured the same outlook and allowed a single

birdstrike certification effort. One of the few differences was in the side windows, which were made smaller in the 757 to achieve the same outside view as the 767, because the narrowbody aircraft's windows were closer to the pilot than those of the widebody.

NEW TWINS ON THE BLOCK

Some 38 months after formal launch, the 767-200 made its maiden flight from Everett on September 26, 1981—four days earlier than the target date originally set in 1979. The first flight, crewed by Tommy Edmonds, Lew Wallick, and John Brit, went reasonably well, apart from problems with the center hydraulic system that prevented the gear from being retracted for the whole flight. A valve in the aircraft's newly developed vacuum flushing toilet system also failed noisily during the flight, the only damage being to the crew's nerves.

The 757 made its maiden flight on February 19, 1982, with John Armstrong in the left seat and Lew Wallick, fresh from the 767 program, acting as copilot. The flight was also the first for the EICAS because the system was not fitted in the 767 until the fifth aircraft. It, therefore, represents something of a milestone in the march toward current cockpit technology and was called into action within minutes of leaving the ground.

The first flight saw a stall on the number two engine, which was running at flight idle. "The first indication of an abnormality was that the EICAS told us we had low oil pressure—at the time we were more interested in the handling qualities of the engine," said Wallick in an interview shortly afterwards with Flight International. "We were reluctant to shut down the engine if we didn't have to. We advanced the throttle, and all 3 rpms [the RB.211 has three spools] came up a little. More throttle increased fuel flow and exhaust gas temperature a little but no more rpm. EICAS confirmed we were outside the windmill-start envelope. It worked just as advertised." A normal air start was carried out, and the 757 landed normally.

Flight tests of the P&W-powered 767, meanwhile, continued unabated, and the aircraft was certificated by the FAA on schedule on July 3, 1982. The GE version followed it two months later. United received its first aircraft on August 19, 1982, and began commercial services with the new 767 on September 8 between Chicago and Denver. As ever, GE was not far behind, and the CF6-powered 767 entered service with Delta on December 15. By the end of 1982 a total of 20 aircraft had been delivered to 6

The 767 played a leading role in creating the phenomenon known as "fragmentation" in the North Atlantic. This was the spread of point-to-point services with long-range twins, which undercut the traditional services operated by high-capacity aircraft on trunk routes connecting major hubs. The effect of fragmentation was not so dramatic in Asia, where the sheer volume of traffic required widebodies of all types. Here a Gulf Air 767-300ER coasts into land by the bustling Kai Tak ramp.

airlines: Air Canada, American, China Airlines, Delta, TWA, and United.

Boeing Field was kept at a hectic pace as the 757 test fleet of five cracked on with the certification effort. The Rolls-powered aircraft was certificated by the FAA on December 21, 1982, followed by the U.K. CAA certification on January 14, 1983. Eastern Airlines took its first aircraft just before Christmas 1982 and put it into service on New Year's Day 1983 between Atlanta and Tampa. The first British Airways aircraft left for England in late January 1983 and entered service from London Heathrow on February 9. The first P&W-powered 757 flew almost one year later and was handed over to Delta on November 5, 1984.

The subsequent years of 757 development were marked by the development of more powerful and reliable engines from both suppliers with the RB.211-535E4B and PW2037/40 representing the top-of-the-range standard by the early 1990s. The engine and airframe reliability and safety standards were so high that the aircraft came to be used by some scheduled and charter operators as almost a 707 replacement on long-range, low-capacity, over-water routes, a role never anticipated by Boeing. The bulk of aircraft were, however, used on the U.S. trunk routes for which they were designed, but only after a faltering start.

Sales were initially disappointing after the first flurry of launch orders. The impact of deregulation in the United States meant that most demand was for smaller aircraft like the 737 to enable operators to increase frequency and meet the competition on hubs and spokes. In addition, fuel prices quixotically fell during the mid-1980s, which resulted in older fleets being kept in service longer. In fact, so bad were these combined effects that only 272 757s were ordered between 1979 and 1987, of which 31 were canceled. However, the long-hoped-for sales boom finally got under way between 1988 and 1989 when 322 aircraft, or 57 percent of total sales, were ordered. The turnaround came about through the imposition of tougher noise rules and the growing congestion at hub airports, where the bigger 757 was becoming more useful than the smaller aircraft it replaced.

The first major derivative, the 757-200PF (Package Freighter) was launched in December 1985 with an order for 20 from United Parcel Service. The PF was virtually identical to the high-gross-weight (250,000 pounds max takeoff) passenger version but had a large 134x86.5-inch cargo door cut into the left side of the forward fuselage together with a new crew door. UPS had ordered 75 -200PFs by 1998. Another derivative, the -200M Combi, sold less well. In fact, by late 1998, only one model had been sold to Royal Nepal Airlines. The -200M, with the same cargo door as the PF but retaining all the passenger features of the standard aircraft, was launched in 1986 and delivered on September 15, 1988.

While the 757 line remained relatively focused on one major version, the 767 family quickly multiplied to include six derivatives by 1993. Like its smaller sibling, the 767 soldiered through a long dry spell in the early 1980s when sales barely kept pace with cancellations. At the start of 1980, sales stood at 166, but by the end of 1985 the net order total had risen by a mere 23. Many orders that survived were also stretched out. American Airlines, for example, originally ordered 30 aircraft for delivery by 1984 but ended up delaying the last 20 for up to five years.

With the recovering global economy, sales began to pick up from 1985 onwards, with the best year being 1989 when 132 orders were booked. Even in the midst of another downturn in 1991, the 767 was Boeing's best-selling aircraft with 83 orders.

In the long tradition of its predecessors, the 767's survival, recovery, and later predominance owes much to the sheer flexibility of the original design. A constant succession of versions with heavier takeoff weight, more fuel, and finally, a longer fuselage ensured that the big twin satisfied multiple markets and prospered in most of them. This is particularly true of the ETOPS revolution, for which the 767 family was primarily responsible. The dramatic explosion of twin-engined jetliner traffic across the North Atlantic can be traced particularly to the first -200ERs.

The baseline 767 design had plenty of margin for growth, which Boeing began almost immediately to exploit. From line number 86 onwards, all 767s regardless of whether they were ordered as ER variants, were built with structural provisions for higher weight and extra fuel tanks. Two ETOPS pioneers, Air Canada and El Al, ordered an initial version of the -200ER with a max takeoff weight of 335,000 pounds (up from the base-line aircraft's 280,000 pounds). Other than some structural strengthening, this version was virtually unchanged from the basic -200. The first major weight and performance jump came with a 345,000-pound MTOW version that was launched in December 1982 with an order for two from Ethiopian Airlines. Unlike the initial ER, this -200ER variant had a larger fuel capacity of 20,450 U.S. gallons compared to the basic aircraft's 16,700 U.S. gallons. The extra fuel was carried in the wing center section, with either two or all three bays converted into fuel tanks.

With the availability of more powerful GE CF6-80C2 and P&W PW4000 engines under development for the 747-400, MD-11, and A300-600 at the time, the weight and range of the -200ER grew even more in late 1986 when Boeing offered a version with a max takeoff weight of 387,000 pounds. The heavy -200ER held 24,140 U.S. gallons of fuel and could fly 216 passengers up to 6,800 nautical miles.

The first stretch version of the 767 was announced as the 300 series in February 1983. Even though no firm customers were lined up for the -300 at the time, Boeing predicted that the natural growth step would greatly increase sales potential. The company was right, and by early 1998 sales of all -300 versions exceeded 550, or more than two-thirds of all 767 sales. Demand for the longer aircraft, which was stretched by 253 inches (21 feet), was so great that by 1997 the only -200 versions on the production line were destined for use as Japanese AWACS. The stretch was accomplished with a 121-inch plug forward of the wing and a 132-inch plug aft, taking overall length to 132 feet, 5 inches. Wingspan, height, and virtually every other feature including the engines were unchanged.

JAL placed the first orders for the -300 in September 1983, followed by Delta in February 1994. The first aircraft, line number 132, flew on January 30, 1986, and was certificated on September 22 of that year.

The -300ER naturally followed quickly on the heels of the basic -300, and the first version, powered by GE CF6-80C2B2 engines was flying by November 1986. Max takeoff weight was soon boosted to an incredible 407,000 pounds for the heaviest versions, almost double the weight envisioned for the 7X7 a scant 10 years before. The heavier -300ERs also presented Rolls-Royce with its first opportunity to offer the RB.211-524G/H engine, which was subsequently certificated in December 1989.

Boeing continued to exploit the 767 and in 1992 began studies of an all-freight version of the 767. This was aimed squarely at UPS, which selected the 767-300F over tough competition from the MD-11F and A300-600F in January 1993. The parcel carrier ordered a staggering 60 -300ER freighters and received its first aircraft in 1995. Apart from the specialized "no frills" freighter ordered by UPS (with no powered cargo system, galley, or freight ventilation), Boeing also offered the "generic" version. This was duly ordered by Asiana of Korea.

The slump of the early 1990s, meanwhile, focused Boeing's mind on new ways to get even more from its large twinjets. As will be discussed in chapter 8, there was plenty of life left in both designs, and both the 757 and 767 were about to put on a new growth spurt.

Cathay Pacific was one of the original group of "working together" airlines that helped define the 777. It was instrumental in pushing for a fuselage width close to that of the 747.

8
Next Generations

As Boeing approached the end of the twentieth century, its aircraft design strategy was profoundly marked by three major events. The company began the decade by launching the 777, which introduced a wave of new methods and technology and was the last all-new widebody design to be produced by any manufacturer in the century. Boeing then decided to focus on the development of derivatives as the best way of meeting market demand in the remaining short-, medium-, and long-haul sectors. The third event resulted from a phase of rapid expansion caused by a booming economy and a series of acquisitions, which culminated in 1997 with Boeing's $16.3 billion takeover of its largest U.S. rival, the mighty McDonnell Douglas Corporation.

These events changed the face of Boeing forever. Together with the aerospace assets of Rockwell North American, which was acquired in 1996, the "new" Boeing became the largest aerospace company in the world. With projected annual revenues of almost $50 billion by the closing years of the decade and more than 215,000 employees, the company suddenly had a bewildering range of products in the civil, military, and space arenas. Almost overnight it had customers in 145 countries, bulging order books, and operations in 27 U.S. states.

Yet, despite the civil order boom and strong prospects in military and space markets, Boeing faced serious problems. It faced massive delivery commitments,

costly restructuring of its newly acquired businesses, and the development of a large range of new products all at the same time. By late 1997 the strain was showing particularly in the civil areas, where deliveries began to slip as Boeing struggled to bring production up to record levels. By early 1998, however, the company once more began to see light at the end of the tunnel. After some serious losses, deliveries caught up, development progressed more smoothly, and the benefits of its big takeovers slowly began to make themselves apparent as the skills and resources of an army of engineers and specialists took effect.

MODEL 777

In many ways the 777 was both the cause and effect of at least two of these profound changes. The 777 was more than just another jetliner to Boeing as it changed the entire way the company designed and produced its products and in doing so led to dramatic changes elsewhere in the industry. These changes were so decisive that they contributed to the takeover of McDonnell Douglas itself.

The 777 program, for example, ushered in a new wave of computer-based design and system technology that had enormous repercussions on Boeing's Joint Strike Fighter (JSF) proposal, a bold venture to reenter the military fighter business on its own terms. The company's renewed confidence in the fighter business

Subtle aerodynamic differences can be seen in the thicker root of the Next Generation's advanced wing. Note also the wider span of the horizontal stabilizer and the wide-chord fan blades of the CFM56-7B engine.

was based on its partnership with Lockheed Martin on the F-22 Raptor. Largely as a result of technology introduced for the 777, the JSF went several steps further, particularly in the low-cost design and manufacturing areas. Boeing's JSF bid, designated the X-32, was chosen in 1996 to compete with Lockheed Martin's X-35 over the proposal submitted by McDonnell Douglas. The loss of the "must-win" JSF contract was one of the major reasons behind the subsequent takeover of McDonnell Douglas by Boeing.

Another key decision that spelled doom for McDonnell Douglas that same year was also directly tied to the damaging success of the 777. In October 1996, McDonnell Douglas decided not to go ahead with a proposed stretched, rewinged derivative of the MD-11 dubbed the MD-XX. After five years of frustration, Douglas Aircraft had finally resolved the early performance problems of the MD-11 but knew that its long-term future depended on a radical redesign. The MD-XX was aimed at the replacement market for 747 "Classics" and was supported by several key carriers such as American, Delta, and Swissair. The MD-XX probably gave Douglas its best, and last, chance to salvage the company's flagging fortunes.

The McDonnell Douglas board decision not to risk the go-ahead of the MD-XX was based on huge development costs and hopeless odds. The company's market share had plummeted through lack of investment in developing a wider range of family members such as a projected four-engined jetliner named the MD-12, and both Airbus and Boeing were reaping the rewards. Airbus was busy designing new long-range derivatives of its A340 series, and Boeing's 777 had quickly overtaken the MD-11, which subsequently became increasingly popular as a freighter.

Although Boeing had great hopes for the 777, which ironically began life as a straightforward DC-10 replacement, it had no idea that it would have such a dramatic impact in so many areas. The project began in late 1986 when Boeing began studying a potential development of its 767 as the basis for a replacement for the large, mainly domestically operated fleets of DC-10s and Lockheed L-1011 TriStars. By December 1989 the 767-X, as it was then called, was quickly turning into an all-new design. "The original intent was a little more capacity and range (than the 767), but as the interest in a bigger aircraft became greater, we started to run into problems with the seven-abreast cross-section of the 767. Stretching it to 200–250 seats also gave us a problem with length. It became obvious that we were going to have to do something with a bigger aircraft," said Mike Bair, former 777 chief project engineer.

In an effort to understand the airline requirements more precisely, Boeing took the innovative step of inviting eight world-class airlines to contribute directly to the design of its "clean-sheet" jetliner. In January 1990 technical representatives from All Nippon Airways, American, British Airways, Cathay Pacific, Delta, Japan Air Lines, Qantas, and United began the first of a series of what became known as "Working Together" meetings with Boeing to thrash out the new shape.

"In designing the new 777, we established a new way of working at Boeing, adopting methods which proved so effective they are being incorporated into programs across the company," said Boeing's Chairman and Chief Executive officer Philip Condit. "For want of a more original phrase, we called this concept 'working

together.' Perhaps a more compelling way to articulate this idea is the favorite saying of a teacher friend of mine, who likes to remind her students that 'nobody is as smart as all of us.'" Condit, who was the original leader of the 777 Division of Boeing Commercial Airplane Group, added ". . . in other words, we airplane designers are very smart, but we become even smarter when we listen to people who are not airplane designers—people like customers and suppliers and professionals from other disciplines within our own company."

In concert with this market-driven approach, Boeing also decided the time was ripe to use advanced computer-based design tools developed by Dassault and IBM. The use of the digital design system CATIA (computer-aided three-dimensional interactive applications), made the 777 the first 100-percent paperless Boeing design.

CATIA offered improved efficiency and cost savings. It linked international suppliers as far afield as Australia, Brazil, Japan, Italy, and England to a single digital database for the aircraft. At its peak, the program involved more than 2,200 workstations and employed the largest mainframe computer network in the world, with eight linked IBM 3090-600J supercomputers that could manipulate around 3 trillion bytes of information. It also cut down expensive "rework" by 65 percent and led to first-time fits between parts that were more accurate than any previous

Another of 34 777s ordered by United makes its nocturnal journey from one part of the Everett final assembly line to another. Still without its Pratt & Whitney PW4084 engines, the 777-222 is joined in the assembly bay by the prototype 777, WA001, which can be seen in the background.

Boeing aircraft. When the first aircraft was assembled, the front section was out of alignment by a mere 0.012 inches vertically and 0.003 inches horizontally. The aft section was out by 0.035 inches vertically and 0.008 inches in the horizontal axis.

As the design came together, Boeing bid the 777 for United's DC-10 replacement program against the A330 and MD-11. Presentations from all the candidates were heard over the weekend of October 12–14, 1990, and United was sufficiently impressed that it selected the 777, ordering 34 with 34 options. As part of the pledge made at the time, Boeing agreed to supply the aircraft "service ready" from day one. It was also designed to be capable of extended over-water flights (ETOPS) at service-ready.

These latter initiatives demanded every aspect of the design be thoroughly tested well before the real aircraft even took to the air. It therefore embarked on development of a $370 million Integrated Aircraft Systems Laboratory (IASL) that did such a convincing job of replicating the 777 that it was called "the skinless aircraft" or "777 Number 0" by Boeing workers. The lab tested 57 major systems, 3,500 line replaceable units and 20,000 additional parts in 70 dedicated test stations, 8 subsystem-integration test facilities, and 3 "super labs." One of these, the system-integration lab, connected the aircraft systems, avionics, flight controls, and cockpit in one giant test rig and was taken for a "flight" several times a day.

The IASL encapsulated the spirit of Boeing's new approach to the 777 design as recalled by Alan Mulally, who was 777 division general manager at the time. "You can simulate it, analyze it, even pray about it, but what you've got to do is build it and test it. So we built in all sorts of things up front—but what we really built was an attitude."

The first 777 was finally unveiled on April 9, 1994, and made its maiden flight on June 12. At first glance the aircraft retained a superficial similarity to the 767 but on closer inspection was totally new in virtually every aspect. The 777 looked a bit like a 767 because it was also a twin-engined, widebody aircraft. Boeing had studied quad and even trijet configurations but dismissed them on grounds of cost and complexity. Based on targets set by the airline working group, it had aimed at achieving 10-percent-better dollars per aircraft-seat-mile costs than the A330 or MD-11. Only a twin could make this target, while a trijet would have suffered from the extra cost of developing a new "Banjo" (shaped) engine fitting in the tail.

"We have no infatuation with twins," said Bair. "We could have done anything we wanted, and we would have. Based on everything we saw, the twin was right." The problem with a twin (as with the four-engined design) was that entirely new engines were required. The quad-jet would have needed new 40,000-pound-thrust class engines, whereas the twin required massive new power-plants capable of pumping out more than 70,000 pounds apiece. The three big engine makers kept close watch on the 777 and were already lined up with new engine designs when the twin was formally adopted.

The fuselage cross-section was also completely new and placed somewhere between the 21-foot, 3-inch-wide 747 and 16-foot, 6-inch-wide 767. Having been told that the 767 was too narrow for the new jetliner, Boeing drew circles around two LD-3 containers and came up with a cross-section of 20 feet, 3 inches. Unlike all its 7-series predecessors, the 777 fuselage was perfectly circular—the first Boeing airliner since the Model 307 to have this feature. The circular section was simpler and stronger and less prone to fatigue than the usual Boeing contoured ellipse. It was also easier to build and lighter because no fairings were needed to smooth out the join between the different radii of the upper and lower sections.

New high-strength aluminum alloys were also used for the first time for the fuselage skin, aft pressure vessel, and stringers, saving 3,200 pounds in weight over more conventional materials. The 777 also used three times the amount of composite materials ever built into any Boeing jetliner. Composites made up almost 10 percent of the aircraft, most of which was in the tail, where the material was used in primary structure for the first time on a Boeing design. The torque box of the vertical stabilizer was built up from carbon-fiber-reinforced materials, while the rudder was made from carbon-fiber epoxy sandwich panels attached to two composite spars and

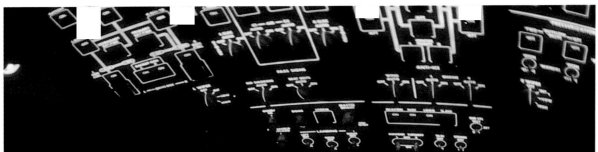

Boeing's most advanced flight deck to date is that of the 777. The design used the 747-400 base-line avionics as a starting point and combined this with the twinjet systems philosophy of the 767. Unlike either, however, it introduced the use of six flat-panel displays developed by Honeywell. The 777 is also Boeing's first fly-by-wire jetliner, though pilot control is maintained through the use of a standard control column rather than the side-stick approach adopted by Airbus.

ribs. Composites were used for moving wing trailing-edge surfaces, spoiler panels, wing fixed leading edges, engine nacelles, root fairings, and landing gear doors, saving a total of 2,600 pounds.

Huge effort went into the design of the 777 wing. True to Boeing standards, the wing was large, with a span of just under 200 feet and an area of 4,628 square feet. Using modified design techniques originally developed for the supercritical 757 and 767 aerofoils, the 777 wing was swept at an angle of just over 31 degrees. Unlike the 767, however, the wing was designed to cruise easily at Mach 0.83. In flight tests, Boeing was pleasantly surprised to find it actually produced cruise speeds of 0.84. This was further improved with the stretched 777-300, which was found to be capable of Mach 0.85.

Like the 757/767 wing, the 777 section was deep in cross-section and generated lift across the full extent of the upper surface rather than in a concentrated area close behind the leading edge. The 777 wing actually produced more lift toward the aft end of the section and was therefore described as "aft-loaded." The wingbox was described by 777 Structures Chief Engineer Larry Rydell as a "carbon copy of the 767 philosophy." The major difference was the "gulling effect inboard on account of the large engines. As the manufacture of the wing involved more automation than anything in the past, we had to work hard with the aerodynamicists to understand and control the curvature of the aerofoil. We couldn't get too carried away on contouring because that's difficult from a formability standpoint." The wing was made up from three torque-box assemblies built up from front and rear spars. In the left and right boxes, the ribs were perpendicular to the rear spar, while the spanwise beams acted as stiffening members in the center box.

The outboard leading-edge slats had a surprising link to a much earlier design, the 727. The design team elected to use the 727-based system because it was much simpler and used few moving parts. It consisted of a one-piece circular-arc slat track, which moved and positioned the slat in one motion. Boeing also dug back into its past for another unusual wing feature. Acting on airline advice, it designed the outer 22 feet of the wing to fold upwards like that of the carrier-based A-6 Intruder aircraft, which it had rewinged. The fold allowed the 777 to fit into DC-10-sized gates at major hubs like Chicago and Dallas/Fort Worth. No operator ordered the folding wing option, however.

In a departure from the traditional four-wheel bogie undercarriage of previous generations, Boeing designed large six-wheel units for the 777. These spread the aircraft's weight more evenly and eliminated the need for a third, or center, main gear leg as developed for aircraft like the DC-10-30 and MD-11. To make steering easier, the aft axle of the gear was articulated and could be steered up to 8 degrees in either direction.

Many more innovations were found beneath the skin of the 777, which was Boeing's first truly digital airliner. The aircraft was provided with fly-by-wire (FBW) flight controls, becoming the first U.S.-made jetliner to use this feature. Boeing had studied FBW for the abandoned 7J7 project but decided to adopt it for the 777 after urgings from airlines like United. The complex systems were also controlled by an electronic "brain" known as the aircraft information management system, or AIMS. This grouped most of the aircraft's essential systems into a single box, including flight management, flat-panel cockpit display control, central maintenance, condition monitoring, engine data interface, and a data conversion highway. Including the AIMS, the 777's avionics and cabin entertainment system contained more than 2.6 million lines of software code compared

By November 1997 virtually all United's 767-operated transatlantic services had been taken over by the growing fleet of 777s. This process reached the West Coast airports like Los Angeles, pictured here, with the advent of the heavy-gross-weight -200IGW versions. Note the letters ETOPS inscribed near the forward cabin door, denoting this aircraft's capability for extended-range twin operations.

The enormous General Electric GE90 turbofans, the world's biggest engines, power the 23 777s ordered by Saudi Arabian Airlines in 1995. This aircraft, pictured here on the delivery ramp at Everett in late 1997, was the first to be delivered later that December.

to 400,000 in the 747-400. Even the cockpit instruments were new-technology active matrix, liquid crystal "flat-panel" displays, which were lighter and more reliable than the cathode ray tube-based option.

EXTENDING THE FAMILY

The inherent flexibility of the big twin quickly became obvious to Boeing, which began to see the 777 as much more than simply a DC-10 replacement. With bigger engines and higher weights, the aircraft could be offered for much longer-range routes, Boeing believed, providing a replacement for 747 "Classics" as well as DC-10-30s and 747SPs. Initial studies focused on a short fuselage 777-100 as well as a stretched 777-300.

The -100X study was aimed at an ultra-long-range aircraft for "thin" routes up to 18 hours long. This proved difficult to justify, however, when the development of more powerful engines meant that the -200 could be developed into just such an aircraft. The added size of the -200 meant this option offered much more attractive seat-mile costs. The first step was the development of an interim -200IGW (increased gross weight) version that could operate transcontinental routes such as Los Angeles to London. Weighing in at up to 648,000 pounds (compared to 545,000 pounds for the initial -200 versions), the -200IGWs quickly became the best-selling version. The first 777-200IGWs, weighing up to 632,500 pounds maximum takeoff weight, began operating in early 1997 with the even higher weight aircraft following a year later.

While studies continued of an ultra-long-range -200X, Boeing quickly developed the stretched -300. Firm configuration was set by October 1995, and first flight took place almost exactly two years later. The 777-300 was a true giant. At 242 feet, 4 inches in length it was longer than a 747 and any jet airliner built before it. Although marginally shorter than the Lockheed C-5 or Antonov An-225, the 777-300 was easily the world's largest twin-engined aircraft as well as the fastest widebody twin. The basic size of the extension was determined by Boeing's tried and tested formula. This was worked out from the 727 onwards and simply said that the -300 would be viable if it carried 20 percent more passengers. Passenger accommodation therefore grew by another 60 seats to a total of 370 in a typical three-class layout while range was pegged at 5,700 nautical miles,

thanks to the 45,220 U.S. gallon fuel-capacity wing tanks developed for the -200IGW.

The result was essentially a 747-100/200-sized aircraft that consumed one-third less fuel and had 40-percent-lower maintenance costs. The stretch was officially launched at the 1995 Paris air show when a group of Asia-Pacific carriers, including three of the original "working together" carriers, signed for 31 aircraft. Boeing hoped the -300 would quickly catch on as the best 747 replacement and forecast that up to 170 stretches could be sold by 2006.

The stretch itself was fairly straightforward, with a 210-inch (10-frame) extension to the forward Section 43 and a 189-inch (9-frame) extension to the aft Section 46. "The decision on a 9-frame stretch for the aft section was based on lift margin, because that was the point where takeoff speeds and rotation margin came together. That allowed us to use the same length landing gear," said 777-200X/300X and former -300 program manager Jeff Peace. The longer aircraft could not rotate as steeply as the -200, meaning that it needed more acceleration to create the same amount of lift for takeoff at equivalent weights.

Other changes included the addition of a standard type-A size emergency evacuation doors and the structural strengthening of the skin and keel beam. This latter part was much bigger in the -300, as it had to absorb the larger body-bending loads. The aircraft also borrowed the retractable tail skid of the 767-300/400 and 757-300 and was fitted with a ground maneuver camera system to help the crew taxi safely. Images from the cameras, mounted beneath the belly and in the horizontal stabilizers, were projected on a T-shaped split screen in the flight deck.

The rapidly paced program was aimed at 32 months from firm configuration to delivery, or roughly three-quarters the time allotted to the -200. Major assembly began in March 1997, and final body join was completed at 1:30 A.M. on the morning of July 21, and the first aircraft was rolled out at Everett on September 8. A "flawless" 4-hour, 6-minute first flight was achieved on October 16, 1997, marking the start of an intensive flight-test program. The first -300 was also powered by Rolls-Royce Trent 892 turbofans, marking a major milestone for the U.K. engine maker. This was the first time non-U.S. engines had powered a Boeing widebody on its first flight and was only the

With
an overall length of 242 feet, 4 inches, the 777-300 is the world's longest jetliner and the biggest twin-engined aircraft in existence. The aircraft was stretched to allow 20 percent more capacity. In passenger terms this equates to 75 more seats in a two-class layout, or a total of up to 451. In a single-class layout, the behemoth will be able to carry up to 550.

second Boeing jet airliner after the 757 to be powered on its maiden flight by Rolls-Royce engines.

The first Pratt & Whitney PW4090-powered aircraft joined the test effort in December 1997, followed by the PW4098-powered test aircraft in early February 1998. The event marked yet another milestone, this being the first flight of the most powerful jet engine yet fitted to this or any other aircraft. The first aircraft was delived in May 1998.

DERIVATIVE DEVELOPMENTS

Following the go-ahead of the 777, Boeing stuck to a policy of derivative development for the rest of the 1990s, beginning with the launch of Next Generation 737 family in January 1994. Despite the remarkable sales success of the "Classic" 737, the growing strength of the Airbus A320 narrowbody family prompted Boeing to begin studies of a next-generation 100- to 200-seater. By late 1993 these had boiled down to five major proposals, of which the simplest was a rewinged 737, dubbed the -X.

Southwest Airlines, one of the advisory airline group members on the 737-X, was convinced that maximum commonality and simplicity were key aspects of the new design and actively pushed Boeing away from high-technology features like FBW flight control. This was a surprise for Boeing, as Airbus actively used FBW as one of the A320's many claimed technical advances over the 737. Other findings were not so surprising. While the airlines wanted high commonality, they also wanted 737 performance, particularly speed, to match or beat the A320. The new jet would have to fly farther, faster, and higher at more economical rates and for lower maintenance costs. Boeing rolled up its sleeves, brushed off its new-found 777-development lessons and set to work. The key to meeting the new performance requirements was a redesigned wing and a new engine.

The advanced wing and powerplant were to be common to all three members of the new family. This included a 737-300X, which was launched as the -700 when Southwest ordered in late 1993 and a stretched version called the -400X that was eventually launched as the -800 by Hapag Lloyd of Germany. The last member was the short-bodied -500X, which was launched as the -600 by SAS of Scandinavia in March 1995 in a major upset of Douglas, which was pushing its MD-95 twinjet.

When the first of the new family rolled out in December 1996, practically the only clue to its identity as

a 737-700 was its much larger "high-speed" wing. Boeing's advisory airlines told it that transcontinental range was vital, as was a higher "sprint" speed of up to Mach 0.82. The wing was therefore increased in area by 25 percent to 1,345 square feet, while span was increased by 18 feet, 2 inches to 112 feet, 7 inches. The increase was achieved by extending the existing tip chord of the current wing and designing an entirely new wingbox. The rear spar was moved aft to provide more room for fuel, and chord increased by around 19 inches, giving a lower thickness-to-chord ratio than the 1960s-vintage design of the original wing. The wider wing held 30 percent more fuel. The new volume of 6,878 U.S. gallons gave the -700 a range of 3,200 nautical miles with up to 128 passengers.

Significantly, the "new 737 is the first Boeing derivative with a new wing," said the Next Generation 737 program manager, Jack Gucker, at the time. The wing was capable of an economical cruise speed of Mach 0.70 at a ceiling of 41,000 feet compared to around Mach 0.74 at 37,000 feet for the Classic. A few more knots of speed were gleaned by using a 777-style raked wing tip and a low-drag aft wing-body join composite fairing around the wing root. The use of an improved CATIA system to design tooling as well as the parts themselves, also improved tolerances and cut the chance of fuel leaks, which had caused some main-

tenance problems on the Classic generation. The wing leading edge was fitted with a new Krueger flap and an additional outboard slat, while the original aircraft's complex triple-slotted trailing-edge flaps were replaced with simpler double-slotted flaps. The redesign reduced parts count, weight, and maintenance costs.

The dorsal fin and vertical stabilizer were lengthened, and the span of the horizontal stabilizer increased to compensate for the increased wingspan and the higher power of the new CFM International CFM56-7B turbofan. The CFM56 had reigned supreme on the 737-300/400 and -500, and the joint GE-Snecma company had no intention of losing this to its arch-rival International Aero Engines. CFMI offered to provide "hundreds of millions of dollars" to share the risk of the venture in return for exclusivity. The gamble more than paid off. By the time the first aircraft were entering service in early 1998 the order book had shot up to a staggering total of more than 900.

The CFM56-7B was vital to Boeing's performance targets. It was designed for 15-percent-lower maintenance costs as well as 8-percent-lower fuel burn. The most visible change was a wide chord fan with swept blades. Internally, it matched the core and low-pressure turbines of the -5B series (used on the Airbus narrowbodies) with a new single-crystal-blade,

he first-ever landing of a 777-300 is recorded in perfect weather at Boeing Field on October 16, 1997. The maiden flight lasted 4 hours and 6 minutes during which the -300 reached a height of 17,000 feet and a maximum speed of 250 knots (Mach 0.54). The flight was also a major milestone for Rolls-Royce, which provided the Trent 892 engines. The -300 was the first Boeing widebody to be powered by a Rolls-Royce engine for its first flight and was only the second company jetliner after the 757 to make its maiden flight powered by non-U.S. engines.

With a maximum operating cruise speed of Mach 0.89, the 777-300 is also the fastest widebody built to date. To check this speed, however, the test team had to dive the giant jetliner at speeds up to Mach 0.96, or roughly Mach 0.02 faster than the -200. The tail-mounted camera is barely visible as a dark spot in the leading edge of the horizontal stabilizer.

The fast-paced 737-700 test effort took a break to include a visit to the 1997 Paris air show. Here the aircraft was displayed as part of a joint demonstration of the Next Generation as both an airliner and a business jet, the BBJ. This also may well have been the first aircraft to be displayed at Paris with a web site address painted on the side!

high-pressure turbine design, a smoother flow path, and more advanced full authority digital engine control.

New avionics and flight deck displays were also available, but here Boeing faced a dilemma. How could it combine demands for commonality, simplicity, and the same type rating with the tempting maintenance and performance benefits of new flat-panel display technology? The answer, surprisingly, was both. A common display system (CDS) was developed using six Honeywell multifunction liquid crystal displays identical to those developed for the 777. The CDS could show the primary fight and navigation data in two formats: electronic flight instrument system (EFIS) or primary flight display/navigation display (PFD/ND). This meant the displays could be tailored to

suit each airline's needs by simply selecting the appropriate format. Southwest, which used 737-300s, -400s, and -500s, wanted EFIS format for commonality. SAS, which became launch customer for the smaller 737-600, adopted the PFD/ND format for similarity with its non-737 fleet types.

Development was swift but not necessarily smooth. The engine's new fan rotor was made from titanium and was therefore 35 percent heavier than its predecessor. The containment of the fan, therefore, needed to be beefed up after tests revealed that blades could puncture the cowling if they became detached at high speeds. The blade retainer itself also needed to be strengthened when several more blades than expected came off in one test. The airframe also had its share of problems, the most serious of which

Key

to the improved performance of the Next Generation 737 was the CFM56-7B turbofan. Complete with a wide-chord, 61-inch-diameter fan and an advanced version of the -3 engine's low pressure compressor, the engine was built to offer up to 8-percent-lower fuel consumption and 15-percent-lower maintenance costs.

was the discovery of vibration in the horizontal stabilizer late on in the flight-test program. The vibration only occurred at very high speeds but was enough to warrant strengthening the structure. The European Joint Aviation Authorities (JAA) also caused Boeing some headaches by insisting on modifications to the over-wing emergency exits to allow European-registered -700 and -800 versions to fly with full loads of 149 and 189 passengers, respectively. A special design team resolved the issue by developing a unique, upward-hinging overwing exit.

Hanging over all these problems was the enormous pressure on the production line caused by the huge increase in orders. The combined effect delayed FAA certification of the -700 from September to November and entry into serv-

ice from October 1997 to January 1998. The delay to the JAA certification was even more pronounced, and the final green light was not given until February 1998. Even this was temporary, pending changes to the speed trim device to meet JAA requirements for increased indication of stall warning to the crew. Despite these problems the Next Generation family was already proving itself to be a huge success and looked set to continue the remarkable story of the 737 well into the twenty-first century.

SIMPLE STRETCHES

Boeing's derivative policy was taken to new lengths, literally, in 1996 and 1997 when two new versions of the 757 and 767 twins were launched in quick succession. Unlike the Next Generation 737, both stretch programs were focused on minimum change. Studies of the stretched 757, dubbed the -300X, began in 1995 and culminated with the launch of the program at the Farnborough air show in September 1996 with an order for 12 from the German charter company Condor.

Design was settled in mid-December, setting the clock ticking on a fast-paced, 27-month effort to deliver the first aircraft by January 1999. This made the -300 timetable the shortest design-to-production and then delivery-cycle time of any Boeing derivative program. Simplicity was key to keeping on track, as was the utilization of techniques developed for the 777 effort and later perfected on the new 737 program. Bruce Nicoletti of

N_{ext}

Generation fuselages were shipped to Renton in one piece from Wichita, Kansas, by rail. The logistics of this operation were enormous when Boeing began shipping the 129-foot-long -800 fuselage, as every tunnel and bridge along the route had to be surveyed for adequate clearance. This process had to be repeated when the decision was taken to develop the even longer -900.

757-300 product marketing described it as a "fly-more-people aircraft." Maximum takeoff weight capability was increased to 270,000 pounds from a maximum of 255,000 pounds on the 757-200. "We've also increased seating capacity by 20 percent, or about 40 passengers. The aircraft will have a 3,500-nautical-mile range capability with that load. That's the main design goal. The extra seating capacity, plus a staggering 48-percent increase in available cargo volume, lowers operating costs dramatically," he said.

Boeing hoped the 757-300 would provide the ideal aircraft for the European charter market and aimed it straight at the heart of the Airbus sphere of influence, where the growing success of the stretched A321-200 was causing concern. The -300 was stretched by 23 feet, 10 inches, making it 178 feet, 7 inches long, or roughly 20 feet longer than the 707-300. This made it the longest narrowbody aircraft ever made by Boeing and the largest aircraft ever made at the Renton site. It was so much longer, in fact, that parts of the factory had to be pushed out, and manufacturing tools were stretched to accommodate it. Despite the changes, Boeing designed it to be built on the same production line as the -200, and the majority of the tooling was common.

The extra fuselage length was not added in the form of plugs; instead, the body sections were extended. Chief Project Engineer Dan Mooney said, "Some of the fuselage panels end up as long as 400 inches. That's single panels, which may present some handling challenges." Body strengthening was concentrated on the overwing Section 44, with increases to skin thickness in the forward Section 43 and aft Section 46. "The horizontal stabilizer will also be beefed up a bit," said Mooney. The gear was also strengthened and the wheels fitted with 26-ply tires to cope with the higher landing speeds and heavier weights. A tail skid was also added, based on the 767-300 design.

The stretch also borrowed elements of the 767 air-conditioning system to cope with the higher-flow requirement of the larger cabin, which was remodeled along the same lines as the 777 and the new 737 family, with sculptured ceilings, indirect lighting, and bigger stowage bins. The -300 was also the first major 757 derivative to benefit from the work of the fuselage assembly improvement team (FAIT). This introduced changes to the manufacturing process as part of Boeing's drive to shorten cycle times from 10 months to around 6. FAIT upgraded the manufacturing process to take advantage of computerized numerical control (CNC) machines. These gradually replaced the conventional build-up tools, which gradually became worn out over time. The

original two-dimensional drawings were scanned into converters to produce CATIA-generated three-dimensional data sets. These were then used by numerical control programmers to develop operating programs for the six CNC machines on the line.

Two of these were used to drill body panels and two to drill stringers, while one drilled body panels and another drilled shear ties. With the holes already made precisely by the CNC machines, the massive tools were no longer needed to hold the assembly in place. Parts virtually snapped together and supported one another during construction.

While plans came together for the next 757, the design of the 767 was evolving again. The company had continued to study further stretches beyond the -300, and in 1997, a full decade after the first flight of the last major derivative, it finally committed to another growth step for the 767. Delta Air Lines launched the new version, which

was dubbed the -400ER with orders and options for up to 70. The -400ER was offered with dual-class seating for 304, compared to 269 for the -300ER. The fuselage was extended 21 feet with plugs fore and aft of the wing, increasing overall length to just over 200 feet.

Maximum takeoff weight was increased to 449,340 pounds and wingspan was enlarged to 170 feet with the addition of new raked tips and extended wing-tip sections. The use of the new tips, which were swept back at more than double the sweep angle but remained in the same plane as the wing, saved almost 2,000 pounds over the winglets that had been previously considered. The higher weights and landing speeds of the -400ER also required the development of a new, high-strength landing gear, which was fitted with 777-style wheels and brakes. The gear was made 19 inches taller to provide more rotation angle for takeoff and landing, and the main gear and trunnion fittings were moved outboard by a few inches to allow it to retract into the same cavity.

The -400ER design was frozen in September 1997, though some important aspects, such as the flight deck, were not hammered out until December. Reacting to airline pressure, Boeing agreed to fit the -400 with an upgraded cockpit based on a mix of the 777 and Next Generation 737. The display architecture was based on the big twin, but the display philosophy followed that of the 737. This display flexibility pilots rated to fly the 757, 767 and 'classic' 737 to use the displays in one format, and pilots rated to fly the 747-400 and 777 to use the same cockpit in another format. Manufacturing was gathering speed in 1998 with a first flight planned for later the following year. Certification and first delivery was due in 2000.

747 DEVELOPMENTS

The long-awaited stretch of the 747, originally planned for the early 1970s, finally looked set to be launched in early 1997. After years of deliberation, Boeing had moved away from the idea of an all-new large airplane (NLA) and focused on maintaining commonality with the existing 747 by developing two new major derivatives, the 747-500X and -600X. Although originally intended to be relatively straightforward stretches, the two slowly evolved into far more ambitious projects using many 777-style features. The two were to share a new wing, an undercarriage, engines, and a FBW flight-control system.

The 250-foot-long -500X was designed to carry 462 passengers on routes up to 8,700 nautical miles, while the longer -600X, at 278 feet in length, was designed to carry up

to 548 in three classes on routes up to 7,750 nautical miles. The maximum takeoff weight for both giants topped the million-pound mark, and each shared a common, advanced 251-foot-span wing. The threat of competition from Airbus was once again a major factor in the process. The European consortium had been actively working on a jumbo program of its own, the A3XX, and Boeing's decision to opt for a derivative rather than a much more expensive all-new design was partially related to gaining a few years' lead on the proposed Airbus. However, the late updates to the 747 derivatives had dramatically upped the development costs to around $7 billion. The knock-on effect was to raise the price to almost $200 million apiece. Airlines suffering from "sticker shock" were also tempted by the promise of highly competitive performance from the A3XX.

While the airlines remained in a quandary, Boeing itself began to have second thoughts. It was worried that the market size was shrinking as a result of a phenomenon called "fragmentation," in which demand for high-capacity aircraft on trunk routes was diluted by the spread of more point-to-point services with smaller aircraft. Boeing only had itself to blame. The 767 and the rapidly growing 777 fleet were prime causes of fragmentation, particularly in the North Atlantic, where the 747 had once ruled supreme. Now it worried that the same thing would happen in the North Pacific, the key market for the two new 747 derivatives. In addition, Boeing had other concerns, including the completion of the Rockwell and McDonnell Douglas mergers and a huge variety of new military and space development efforts. To cap it all, the company was pushing the 767-400ERX, as it was still called in early 1997 and two new versions of the 777, the -200X and -300X.

Despite the omens, the aerospace world was still shocked when Boeing called a halt to the 747-500X/600X programs on January 20, 1997. "We just could not make a business case for it," said Mike Bair, then vice president of product strategy and marketing. "The small size of the market meant the amount of money we'd have had to spend, with or without fragmentation, just did not make sense."

As the dust settled, Boeing went back to studying more modest increased gross weight developments. The first of these, the 747-400X achieved firm design configuration in May 1998 and provided the first significant growth step toward a one-million-pound aircraft. The -400X had a maximum takeoff weight of 910,000 pounds and a range of up to 7,700 nautical miles. Qantas, the Australian flag-carrier, was interested in the new variant to overcome

The enlarged span of the Next Generation's 112-foot, 7-inch-wide wing is one of the only easily identifiable changes to the appearance of the aircraft. One of the test -700 fleet is pictured on landing at Boeing Field. The -700 first flew in February 1997 and was certificated by the FAA on November 7 that year after the four flight test aircraft conducted more than 1,550 flights, 2,200 hours of ground tests, and 2,000 hours of flight tests. Late structural changes to the stiffness of the horizontal stabilizer added a month to the program and delayed first deliveries to Southwest by roughly the same period.

The main gear of the Next Generation was made slightly taller as a result of changes to the wing, which was slightly "gulled" near the root. The gear itself was also modernized with new wheels and tires.

payload/range restrictions on some of its major transpacific routes and hoped to take the first around the year 2000. The -400X incorporated structural strengthening around the center body, wing-to-body join, wings, flaps, and landing gear. It was also provided with belly fuel tanks to boost range beyond 7,000 nautical miles.

For the future, Boeing hoped the -400X might provide the first building blocks for the progressive and cost-effective expansion of the family. The fear of the A3XX remained, despite the sudden economic crisis in Asia and the decision by Airbus to slow down the development of the new jumbo while it concentrated on A340 derivatives.

By early 1998 one of Boeing's most promising studies was defined as the -400Y. Incorporating a 31-foot stretch, the -400Y was sized to seat around 500 passengers and fly 7,500 nautical miles. Other than the stretch, which consisted of two plugs fore and aft of the wing, the major feature of the Y was the insertion of two 90-inch plugs in the root of each wing. These increased fuel capacity sufficiently to maintain -400 range capability and extended overall wingspan to 226 feet.

Other derivatives still under consideration included a simpler 20-foot stretch with capacity for 495 passengers, and the -400LRX. This rather strange option reverted to the original 747-200 upper deck but retained the higher-weight wing, systems, and other features of the -400F freighter. The combination provided capacity for 375 passengers on routes more than 8,000 nautical miles and was clearly offered as an alternative to Airbus Industrie's newly launched A340-500 and -600 derivatives.

NEW HORIZONS

As 1997 came to a close, one of Boeing's biggest concerns was what to do with the newly acquired Douglas product line. It was no great surprise when it announced in November 1997 that it would close down the venerable MD-80 line. News of the closure of the more advanced MD-90 twinjet was slightly more perplexing until, the following week, Boeing announced the launch of yet another 737 derivative of almost exactly the same size. The MD-90 was widely acknowledged as one of the quietest airliners in existence and was only into its third year of full production when the ax fell.

The 737-900 was launched in late 1997 with a $1 billion-plus order from Alaska Airlines for 10 plus 10 options. The fuselage was stretched with a 42-inch plug behind the wing and a 63-inch plug forward, providing room for up to 15 more passengers. This allowed up to 177 passengers to be carried in a two-class layout, although requirements for emergency exits meant maximum seating could not go beyond the 189 seats already configured for the -800. The latest stretch meant that Boeing's "baby" 737 was now 138 feet long, or larger than the first 707 models! The -900 was aimed squarely at the Airbus A321 and, initially, the MD-90 itself. Deliveries to Alaska were expected to begin in 2001.

Another surprise of Boeing's product strategy review was the decision to maintain the MD-11 in production. Sales of the big trijet had slowed to a trickle and dried up altogether with the imminent takeover by Boeing. However, the MD-11 had begun to shine as an outstanding

German operator Hapag Lloyd was destined to receive the first -800 in 1998 following completion of European JAA certification requirements that entailed the design of a new upward-hinging emergency overwing exit door. At the time of the delivery the price of the -800 ranged from between $48 million to $54 million, depending on options.

freighter, and as recently as 1996, carriers like Lufthansa had placed orders at the expense of Boeing's own 767-300F alternative. However, by mid-1998, no more orders had been taken and Boeing finally decided to axe the MD-11.

Boeing kept the biggest surprise of all to last when it announced the future of the MD-95 twinjet in January 1998. The fate of the small jetliner had been in the balance for some time as its only customer was the low-cost operator ValuJet. Following an accident in 1996, the airline had changed its name by merging with another carrier to become AirTran Airlines but remained committed to the MD-95. While Boeing was expected to honor the airline's contract with Douglas, no one was sure if it would continue to support the effort or simply write it off and concentrate on sales of its similarly sized 737-600. As a condition to pursuing further development, it asked every supplier to reduce its costs.

It therefore came as something of a shock when Boeing not only guaranteed full commitment to the future development of the aircraft but renamed it the Boeing 717. Although this designation had been given to the KC-135 and briefly the 720 (717-020), the 717 was now given to the small twin because this represented a "100-seater." It also stressed Boeing's wholehearted

support of the aircraft and, therefore, added to its market credibility. It was clear that Boeing had decided to adopt the MD-95 as its best bet to enter the regional jet market. It estimated the market potential at around 2,500 over the next 20 years and believed that if it could act quickly, the 717 could snap up most of this before the competition was in place.

The regional jet market was in some state of confusion at the time, with none of the other embryonic projects near fruition. Fokker had collapsed two years before, and British Aerospace, which built the Avro RJ—the only other similarly sized aircraft—had thrown in its lot with Aerospatiale and Aeritalia in the AI(R) Aero International (Regional) partnership. Just before the 717 announcement, AI(R) had decided against a new regional jet project, the AI(R) 70. Another regional aircraft manufacturer, Saab, had just announced it was getting out of the business, and regional jet makers in Brazil, Canada, and Germany were focused on smaller products. The only brand-new designs likely to compete directly were the Indonesian N2130 and the slow-moving AE31X project (involving Airbus Industrie Asia, Aviation Industries of China, and Singapore Technologies). With the collapse of so many Asian economies in late 1997, uncertainty continued to dog the AE31X project. In February 1998, Airbus itself added to the confusion by

A_s Boeing stepped up production to meet a huge surge in demand in 1997, the pressure threatened to overwhelm the line as parts shortages began to occur. Some completion work was moved outside while the production line was "rebalanced," and no new aircraft were introduced onto the line for 25 days to give suppliers a chance to catch up. The disruption affected both "Classic" and "Next Generation" 737s, like those shown here.

revealing studies of a shortened A319, dubbed the M5, to compete head-on with the 717.

For the immediate future Boeing concentrated on developing the initial version, now called the 717-200, for AirTran. The first 9 were due to be delivered from the Long Beach production line in California in 1999. Boeing hoped that production would eventually reach up to 10 aircraft per month and sketched out plans for new derivatives, the 80-seat 717-100 (formerly called the MD95-20) and the 120-seat 717-200 (MD95-50). Virtually the entire production of structures and components was undertaken by risk-sharing partners. Korean Air and Hyundai supplied the nose and wings, respectively, while other major components came in from Germany, Israel, Japan, Taiwan, and the United States. The engine maker BMW Rolls-Royce was a major partner with 20 percent of the program, and it supplied its BR715 engine on an exclusive basis.

To meet the needs of the future, Boeing was once again looking at very large aircraft as well as supersonic transports. One of the most promising large aircraft concepts was acquired with McDonnell Douglas and was called the Blended Wing Body (BWB). This was essentially a form of flying wing with a blended-in fuselage. Initially unveiled as a study by McDonnell Douglas in 1996 before its takeover, the BWB had double-deck seating for up to 800 and a wingspan of around 290 feet. The outstanding feature of the design was its inherently superb aerodynamics, which made it very efficient. NASA was sufficiently interested to undertake tests of a scale model at NASA Ames with Stanford University in 1997. Following the takeover, Boeing immediately sent a design team to Long Beach, where it studied the configuration.

Several major problems remained, however, including ground infrastructure issues for loading and unloading, as well as passenger acceptability of what would be a predominantly windowless aircraft. Parallel studies of other large aircraft concepts therefore remained along more traditional lines, although some new concepts included high-wing configurations previously reserved for cargo transports.

Against this background the ever-present lure of supersonic speeds continued to attract some attention from Boeing, which was a major player in NASA's High-Speed Research (HSR) program. This effectively concentrated the best elements of U.S. industry and university research into one combined effort to develop the technol-

The first 737-600 is seen on the Renton final assembly line at far right with the Boeing colors on the fin. The -600 made a successful 2-hour, 28-minute first flight on January 22, 1998, on the same day that total orders for the Next Generation family climbed to 811. Just four months later they passed the 900 mark.

OPPOSITE
By January 1998 Boeing had firmed up the configuration of the 767-400ER, which will be 21 feet longer than the -300. The main changes included an all-new flight deck combining elements of the Next Generation 737 and 777, a new 777-style interior, and a larger 170-foot, 7-inch wingspan. The increase was made with composite raked-tip extensions supported on metal spars. Unlike the winglets originally planned, the extensions were in-plane with the wing but were raked back at virtually twice the sweep angle. The first 767-400 was set for rollout in August 1999, and first deliveries were due to begin to Delta in 2000.

ogy for an economic and, above all, environmentally acceptable replacement for the Anglo-French Concorde. The eventual High-Speed Civil Transport (HSCT), if built, would be a 300-plus seater with a range of at least 5,000 nautical miles. With a projected speed of Mach 2.4, the HSCT would cut the average journey time from Los Angeles to Tokyo from 10.3 to 4.3 hours.

For the immediate future, however, Boeing will concentrate on the subsonic commercial arena, where it has reigned supreme for nearly half a century. With a vastly expanded product range and up to 10 new civil derivatives either entering service or in the early design stage, the company seems in better shape than ever to face the challenges of the twenty-first century.

Boeing took much of the aerospace world by surprise when it renamed the MD-95 the 717 following its takeover of McDonnell Douglas. The 717 spearheads its attack on the upper end of the growing regional jet market and will be led by the -200 version, one of which is pictured here in final assembly at Long Beach, California. The first 717 flew in 1998, and production was expected to ramp up to as much as 10 aircraft per month by the early part of the twenty-first century.

Land of the giants. Much of the future growth of the 747 by 1998 depended on the recovery of the faltering Asian economies. The rapid growth of the region had fueled 747 sales for more than a decade, as illustrated in this shot of the packed Kai Tak ramp at Hong Kong.

Appendix Production by Model 1916-1998

Model	Designation	Number Built	Production Dates
1	B&W	2	1916
2	C	1	1917
3	C	3	1917
4	EA	2	1917
5	C	52	1918
6	B-1	9	1918–1928
7	BB-1	1	1919
8	BB-L6	1	1920
10	GA-1/2	12	1920
15	PW-9, FB-1	123	1923–1928
16	DH-4, 02B-1	298	1920–1925
21	NB-1/2	77	1923–1927
40	40	77	1925–1932
42	XCO-7	3	1925
50	PB-1	1	1925
53	FB-2	2	1925
54	FB-4	1	1926
55	FB-3	3	1925–1926
58	XP-4	1	1926
63	TB-1	3	1927
64	64	1	1926
66	XP-8	1	1927
67	FB-5	27	1926–1927
68	AT-3	1	1926
69	F2B-1	35	1926–1928
74	XF3B-1	1	1927
77	F3B-1	73	1928
80	80	15	1928–1930
81	XN2B-1	2	1928
83	XF4B-1	1	1928
89	XF4B-1	1	1928
93	XP-7	1	1928
95	95	25	1928–1929
96	XP-9	1	1930
99	F4B-1	27	1929
100	100	8	1929–1932
101	XP-12A	1	1929
102	P-12/-12B	99	1929–1930
103–199	used for Boeing-designed aerofoil sections		
200	Monomail	1	1930
202	XP-15	1	1930
203	203	7	1929–1936
204	204	2	1929
205	XF5B-1	1	1930
214	Y1B-9	1	1931
215	YB-9	1	1931
218	218	1	1930
221	Monomail	1	1930
222	P-12C	96	1931
223	F4B-2	46	1931
226	226	1	1930

Model	Designation	Number Built		Production Dates
227	P-12D	35		1931
234	P-12E	110		1931–1932
235	F4B-3/4	113		1931–1933
236	XF6B-1	1		1933
246	Y1B-9A	5		1932–1933
247	247	75		1933–1935
248	XP-936/P-26	3		1932
251	P-12F	25		1932
256	F4B-4	14		1932
264	YP-29	3		1934
266	P-26A/B/C	136		1934–1935
267	267	9		1933
273	XF7B-1	1		1933
281	281	12		1934–1935
294	XB-15	1		1937
299	B-17	6,981 Boeing 5,745 Douglas and Vega		1935–1945
307	Stratoliner	10		1938–1940
314	Clipper	12		1938–1941
344	XPBB-1	1		1942
345	B-29, B-50	3,138 Boeing 1,204 Bell and Martin		1942–1953
367	C-97	888		1944–1956
377	Stratocruiser	56		1947–1950
400	XF8B-1	3		1944–1945
450	B-47	1,373 Boeing 667 Douglas and Lockheed		1947–1956
451	XL-15, YL-15	12		1947–1948
464	B-52	744		1952–1962
500–599	used for industrial products			1946–1968
600–699	used for missiles			1947–1976
707	707-	1,013		1956–1992
717	KC-135A/B, C-135A/B, and former McDonnell Douglas MD-95* (717-200)	806 55		1956–1965 *1997–
720	720	154		1959–1968
727	727-100/200	1,832		1962–1984
737	737-100/200/300/400/500/600/700/800/900	3,060	4,041*	1967–
747	747-100/20/300/400/SP	1,155	1,305*	1968–
757	757-200/300/C-32A	802	920*	1983–
767	767-200/300/400 E-767 AWACS	701	828*	1983–
777	777-200/300	133	392*	1994–
901	YQM-94A Compass Cope (UAV)	2		1973
953	YC-14	2		1976

*unfilled announced orders as of June 1998

INDEX